I0793114

Praise for *Brother Al Stricklin Now*

As rollicking and jaunty as an Al Stricklin piano solo, David Stricklin's full-bodied portrait of his father is as good a description as we have of how the legendary Bob Wills and His Texas Playboys managed to transform the hardest circumstances into good times for a generation of Southwesterners and beyond. Read this book and get up and dance!

Stephen R. Tucker
Music historian

For Al, becoming a Texas Playboy marked the beginnings of a lifelong friendship with Bob Wills. Theirs was a friendship that included their families, one I am happy to say continues even now. As my father's friend, Al spent time talking, laughing, trusting, staying in touch, and sharing in ways that meant so much to my father and to my family.

Al's musical genius, performance style, and devotion to Bob, the band, and those who came to hear them remain remarkable, things this book depicts so well.

Carolyn Wills
Daughter of Bob Wills and Executive Director of the Bob Wills Heritage Foundation

David Stricklin's deft study of his celebrated father is a delectable three-layer-cake of a story—personal memoir, band biography, and cultural history rolled into one. With its separate themes blended through time, the narrative unfolds organically, revealing the author's own love of Western Swing. The result is both fascinating and relatable, moving and meaningful. It's just a GREAT story from every angle. As a reader, I couldn't put it down. A delighted listener, I'm right there on the piano bench with Al.

Leanne Langley
Historian and writer

BROTHER
AL STRICKLIN NOW

Also by David Stricklin:

A Genealogy of Dissent: Southern Baptist Protest in the Twentieth Century

Southern Music/American Music, Revised and Expanded Edition, with Bill C. Malone

Louis Armstrong: The Soundtrack of the American Experience

BROTHER AL STRICKLIN NOW

Memories of a Texas Playboy

DAVID STRICKLIN

TCU PRESS
Fort Worth, Texas

Library of Congress Cataloging-in-Publication Data

Names: Stricklin, David, 1952- author
Title: Brother Al Stricklin now : memories of a Texas Playboy / David Stricklin.
Description: Fort Worth, Texas : TCU Press, [2026] | Includes bibliographical references.
Identifiers: LCCN 2026021993 | ISBN 9780875659770 paperback | ISBN 9780875659787 ebook
Subjects: LCSH: Stricklin, Al, 1908-1986 | Wills, Bob, 1905-1975 | Texas Playboys | Country musicians--Texas | Western swing (Music)--History and criticism | LCGFT: Biographies
Classification: LCC ML417.S92 S77 2026 | DDC 786.2/1642092--dc23/eng/20260512
LC record available at https://lccn.loc.gov/2026021993

TCU PRESS

TCU Box 298300
Fort Worth, Texas 76129
www.tcupress.com

To my niece, Leigh Anne Willis Bedrich, and my nephews, Jerry Carl Willis and Robert Andrew Willis, who loved their grandfather Al and loved his music

Contents

Acknowledgments

I would like to thank my family and friends, who have heard and told much of what is in here, especially Sally Browder, Annie Stricklin and John Drymon, Sarah Stricklin and Adam Wilkerson, Nancy Stricklin Willis and her kids, to whom the book is dedicated, and Judy Stricklin and Audrey Black. Annie did a particularly helpful reading that drew on her excellent skills as an editor. Thanks also to dear friends who have loved these stories and contributed to them, especially Landa Sloan Orrick (who appears in these pages as "Little Friend Linda") and Michael Jay Dohoney. Leanne Langley and Steve Tucker read the manuscript and made very helpful comments. Thanks also to David Fleming for taking a look and giving some good advice.

Two Little Rock friends, Carmie Henry and the late Billy Roy Wilson, urged me to write this book. I thank Carmie and wish I could thank Judge Wilson. Deep gratitude goes to two of my former professors, the late Tom Charlton from Baylor days and Bill Malone from Tulane. Tom went against the grain and told me decades ago that it was okay to write about vernacular music, even dance bands, and that he would take the heat for it from the stuffier precincts of the university, which he did, inspired in large part by his old UT-Austin seminar mate, Bill Malone, who almost singlehandedly made writing about commercial country music an accepted practice in the academic world. Bill's extraordinary knowledge and integrity are standards any writer would be delighted to share. Speaking of Baylor, a little posthumous thanks should go to President S. P. Brooks, who kicked my father out of Baylor for playing a dance at the Knights of Columbus Hall in Waco. As you will see, that was the best thing that ever happened to him.

Great appreciation goes to Carolyn Wills and all the gang at the Bob Wills Heritage Foundation. I always enjoy introducing Carolyn to people by saying, "My dad used to work for her dad." Her love for and commitment to this story are unbounded. Thanks to Brett Bingham, who connects with it in so many ways, including as the manager of the current version of the Texas Playboys. Jim Haber (Floyd Domino) has been part of my family since he and Al met in the 1970s. My sisters and I love him like a brother, just as Betty and Al loved him like a son. Thanks also to Ray Benson, who has kept western swing and the Bob Wills legend alive for so many people, and to Cindy Roberts, who does the same thing. Thanks to H. K. Stewart for good advice and to William Williams, Dan Williams, and all the fine people of TCU Press. They are a delight to work with.

This book is in large part the result of a lunch conversation in Little Rock with Judge Raymond Abramson and longtime Arkansas newspaper columnist John Brummet. The judge got us together so I could tell Brummett Bob Wills and Al Stricklin stories, after which he said, "You should write a book about all this." I said, "You're about the five hundredth person who's told me that." And Brummett said, "Well, put me down for number 501." So I figured I had to do it.

Finally, thanks to all fans of Bob Wills and His Texas Playboys, who created and lived this story along with the guys in the band. Their devotion helped get the story started. Even now, that devotion keeps it going strong.

CHAPTER 1
Invitation

One day in the spring of 1974, my father called and asked me to go with him to Austin on what he thought at the time might be kind of a wild goose chase. I was a senior at Baylor University in Waco and always up for a road trip. And his description of what he was getting himself into, though vague and a little confused, sounded interesting.

He said, "I got a call from somebody in a band down there. 'Stuck in a Tree' or 'Dead in the Ditch.' Something like that."

"Asleep at the Wheel?" I asked.

"Hey, that's it," he replied.

They had invited him to drive down from his home in Cleburne, just south of Fort Worth, and sit in with them at a show they were booked to do at the Ritz Theater on Sixth Street. He said, "I don't know about this. They sound like a bunch of hippies. I think I might need a bodyguard." I said I'd go, of course. He picked me up at my apartment a few days later, and off we went.

Asleep at the Wheel and other pathbreaking bands in Austin were on the way then to becoming a very big deal. I had been following the development of these new groups of mostly young musicians, especially through a college friend, Dennis Keys, who connected me to a network of Texas coffee houses—including the Rubaiyat in his hometown of Dallas—where performers could try out songs and work on arrangements. He and I went to the Rubaiyat several times and heard Michael Martin Murphey, Steve Fromholz, and others and went to the Armadillo World Headquarters in Austin and saw what a lot of people then called the "Austin Interchangeable Band." Mostly, this music was termed "progressive country" and in a sense was bridging the gap between "longhairs" and "rednecks," a gap that had been a big source of tension in the 1960s. You could get in a fight in a hurry if you had long hair and wandered into a bar where the jukebox was stocked with George Jones and Patsy Cline, as memorialized in "Uneasy Rider" by Charlie Daniels and other tunes originating from either side of that line, criticizing the folks on the other side of it. Merle Haggard's songs "Okie from Muskogee" and "Fightin' Side of Me" added to that feeling. But here they were in Austin, longhairs playing steel guitars and fiddles, sounding somewhat like country music. Not exactly the way Gram Parsons and the Flying Burrito Brothers had done a little earlier with country-rock and not at all making fun of country music. To the extent it was "progressive" depended on your point of view, and Murphey got irate when his picture ended up on the cover of Jan Reid's book about a lot of this, *The Improbable Rise of Redneck Rock*, saying, "I'm not a redneck, and I don't play rock music." Whatever it was, it was fun to listen to, and a lot of us loved going to Austin and other places to hear it. What Asleep at the Wheel was doing, though, was a little different, which my father and I realized, in separate ways, when we got to the Ritz Theater.

He had invited a friend of many decades, Manley Head, to meet us at the show. Manley was a lawyer and dealmaker in Austin who was very familiar with the local music scene that was then in the early stages of becoming the powerhouse that made Austin internationally famous. We got to the theater just in time for the show. Manley and I found seats as my dad was rushed backstage. After a few minutes of a Johnny Mack Brown movie, Asleep at the Wheel came on and played several numbers. I had heard that they were doing some interesting work in reviving western swing, swing music played mostly with instruments usually found in "western" bands. But I didn't know a lot about how they went about it, let alone how good they were, which was very good. After the third or fourth song, the band's leader, Ray Benson, said to the crowd, which apart from Manley Head and me seemed to be mostly University of Texas students, "Folks, we have a special treat for you today. One of the legends of western swing, the original piano player from the great Bob Wills and His Texas Playboys, Brother Al Stricklin!"

The place exploded.

When he walked out onto that stage and saw and heard the reaction of all those kids, my father was—I think you have to say—stunned. At the time, he was sixty-six years old. Though he had stayed active as a musician the entire time, it had been thirty-two years since he had played fulltime with Bob Wills, longer probably than ninety percent of the people in that theater had been alive. Bob himself hadn't performed since the first of a series of strokes in 1969. Merle Haggard had released a Bob Wills tribute album in 1970, but not many young people back then paid Haggard much attention, partly because of his "Okie from Muskogee" vibe. Nobody realized at the time that Haggard's 1970 album foreshadowed the rebirth of interest in Wills and his band. He hosted a gathering of old Playboys at his home in Bakersfield in 1971 and included Al. Then, most of the original band members who were able to get together recorded an album in December 1973, *Bob Wills and His Texas Playboys: For the Last Time*, which became a big seller. But none of this was well known among the younger set.

Until that moment, it seemed most likely to my father that the vast majority of young people in Texas, or anywhere else, didn't have a clue who Bob Wills was, let alone Al Stricklin. But here they were, yelling their heads off. I had seen him perform many times, and he was always comfortable in front of a crowd. But this was different. It was the first time I had ever seen him shocked by getting a look at the people who were about to hear him play the piano. He quickly recovered, took his place on the piano bench, and gave the inspired performance he'd been asked to give. But the experience of seeing how excited these young people were to see him and hear him play made a deep impression on him, to say the least.

As it happened, the members of Asleep at the Wheel weren't hippies. But they were young, in their twenties, wearing western clothing, cool but lively. They had an old-fashioned way of engaging their audience that was very different from the way a lot of rock bands acted, which was aloof, sometimes even bored, but eager nonetheless to impress people with how well they played. Everybody in Asleep at the Wheel seemed highly skilled, talented, and gutsy, but they also seemed more interested in making sure everyone at the show had a good time than they were in showing off. That right there, if nothing else, won my dad over. If he had had any doubts about this group of young musicians, those doubts went out the window immediately because that idea—that the point of music was to create enjoyment, not impress people—was the driving force for my father's entire life as a musician, as it had been for his old boss from 1935 to 1942, Bob Wills. What impressed me was that Ray Benson and his bandmates were spending time at their shows telling these young people where their music came from. It was all kind of amazing.

And it turned out that the time my father spent backstage with Asleep at the Wheel at the Ritz Theater before they went on was something of a reunion, following up on a 1973 meeting at the disc jockey convention in Nashville. He hadn't put together till then that the musicians he had met in Nashville were the ones who invited him to come down and play with them in Austin. So, this was the second time he had met the Wheel's great piano player, Jim Haber—known professionally as Floyd Domino—who became one of my father's most treasured friends. Al and Jim didn't have much time to talk before the Ritz Theater show, but what my dad and I talked about after the show was the amazing fact that a new generation of fans knew about the Texas Playboys. When he got back to Cleburne, he called a couple of his old friends from the original band, Smoky Dacus and Joe Ferguson, and said, "You guys won't believe this, but there's a bunch of young people who know who we are!" Smoky had stayed in the business, mainly as the manager of a radio station in Rogers, Arkansas, and Joe had continued to perform in the Fort Worth area, where he was living. But they were just as astonished as my father was to learn that they'd been "discovered" by a new generation of fans.

The coming together of all these things—Asleep at the Wheel's influence on a new audience of young people, the rise of Austin as a music center rivaling Nashville, Haggard's love of Bob Wills, Bob's death in 1975, and a partnership between a new group made up of original Texas Playboys and Bob's widow, Betty Anderson Wills—brought about a remarkable second act for the Texas Playboys. That second feature connected the "glory years" of Bob and the pre-World War II band and a base of fans that included folks who remembered them from the first time and those who were just discovering them. People on various parts of this timeline found their way into the story in a variety of ways.

For instance, when I was growing up in Cleburne, if people asked me about my parents, Betty and Al Stricklin, I would usually say, "My mother is a bookkeeper, and my father is a piano player with a day job." As I got older, and especially in the last few decades, if the people asking about my parents wanted to know more about the piano player, I would mention that he played with Bob Wills and His Texas Playboys from 1935 to 1942 and then again for about ten years when the band got back together after Bob's death in 1975. At that point, the people always separated themselves into two groups, the clueless or the ecstatic. Some would nod politely but blankly. That meant they didn't know about Bob Wills and His Texas Playboys: the clueless. People in the other group, the ecstatic, usually said something along the following lines: "Are you serious? The Texas Playboys! Holy cow! That's fantastic!" Then, excited questions followed, and sometimes the simple question about my parents turned into a long conversation about my father's time in the celebrated band. Along the way, the bookkeeper usually fell out of the conversation. In a sense, that was only natural. Anybody really excited about the chance to hear about the life of one of the original Texas Playboys was probably not that interested in hearing much about the life of someone who kept the books at a drugstore, though that drugstore deserves a book of its own. What a collection of characters!

But this account of memories of the piano player includes memories of the bookkeeper. It's impossible to understand him without understanding her. She was a character in her own right, and she had a big influence on him, in all the ways married people do, but also on his career, his music, and the somewhat modest fame he enjoyed at two different points in his life. She had a mixed attitude toward his fame. Sometimes it seemed like resentment. Sometimes it seemed like appreciation, even excitement. There was the inevitable annoyance at fans who wanted to buttonhole him and slow them down as they were trying to go someplace. But there was the pleasure of meeting celebrities, including some very famous people. One of the greatest gifts was the friendship of Jim Haber/Floyd Domino. Jim had affectionate relationships with both of them, to the point that my sisters —Nancy Stricklin Willis and Judy Stricklin—and I consider him our adopted brother. Probably the closest our mother ever came to having a fistfight was during an encounter with Jim's actual mother, as they both tried to claim credit for him at an awards ceremony in California. He likes to tell how Betty enjoyed saying she had two sons six months apart. He sat with our family at the funerals of both of my parents. He and his memories will figure prominently in this story.

Al lived to be seventy-eight years old and worked with Bob Wills for not quite seven of those years. You might say those years with Bob Wills were the most important of his life. They surely were the most exciting. They defined who he was in many respects, but there was a lot more to his life, some of which has found its way into these pages. But this isn't a biography of Al Stricklin. It's a book of memories, both memories he shared with my sisters and with me and those we have of direct experiences with him. I tried to check facts I thought needed checking, especially when one of my memories didn't line up with those of my sisters. Some of these memories come from the book he wrote, *My Years with Bob Wills*. Others come from interviews he did, some with me. And I know that in some cases his memories were a little out of sync with those of other people. I doubt there are many instances where that matters much, and not because of the old yarn-spinner's advice: "Never let the truth get in the way of a good story." But I know that sometimes memory plays tricks. Over the years, my niece and nephews—Leigh Anne Willis Bedrich, Jerry Willis, and Robert Willis—have shared with me their own memories of Al as a grandfather, fishing buddy, and family comedian. All of these memories of a Texas Playboy, his and ours, I've tried to represent faithfully without necessarily knowing exactly whose memories are whose. Families are like that, and memory is complicated, just as his life was. His story is a lot about getting a chance to do something great early in his life, but also about getting a second chance to do it again, which in many ways saved him from what could have been a sad ending.

He was a fun guy whose life wasn't always fun, a man of many talents who sometimes had to use some of those talents to do work he didn't care for much, such as selling things. But I never knew of anyone who didn't like him. Like everybody, but I think especially musicians and other artists, he was the product of a lot of experiences and influences, some delightful and some pretty dreadful. But they all pointed him, in one way or another, to a life of creativity and joy as a piano player and as an entertainer. I never saw him or anyone else have a bad time when he sat down at a piano. How he got to be the guy on the piano bench is a story with deep roots in the rich soil of American music.

CHAPTER 2
Antioch

Alton Meeks Stricklin was born in January 1908 on a farm in Johnson County, Texas, a few miles northwest of the town of Grandview, next to the farm of his mother's family, the Bentons. The community where the Stricklins and Bentons had their land was known as Antioch, and it consisted of a few farms, a rural school, and a cemetery. Alton's father, Zebedee Meeks Stricklin—who went by Meeks—and Meeks's brothers Tom (James Thomas) and Jack (Andrew Jackson), the youngest of that generation of Stricklin children, came to Texas from West Tennessee at various points in the 1890s. Alton used to tell about how Meeks and Tom went back to Tennessee to get Jack loose from some trouble he had run into with the law, offenses that were always described in the family as just boyish pranks but worrisome enough that they had landed Jack in the care of the State of Tennessee. One good result of that experience was that Jack learned a good bit about being a printer. Once back in Texas, Tom spotted an ad for a printing press and newspaper for sale in the Texas Panhandle town of Brownfield and offered to loan Jack the money to buy it. That did the trick, and Jack straightened up just fine and ended up being the publisher of the paper and a successful and highly regarded member of the community, as shown by his election as a delegate to the 1920 Democratic Party state convention, which in those days was quite a feather in one's cap. Tom was a popular schoolteacher and Church of Christ preacher. Meeks bought some land and took to farming. All three brothers had been brought up in "the Church," which was how everybody who was a member of a Church of Christ congregation referred to it.

One of the Stricklin family's favorite stories starred Uncle Jack in one more supposed act of mischievous fun. Before he set out to make his way in the newspaper world, he stayed with Meeks on the farm for a while. This was probably in the middle part of the 1890s, somewhat after the time when "camp" meetings were a common feature of the religious life of the American frontier. Some people called them "protracted" meetings because they lasted for several days. In areas such as the countryside around Grandview, which had several fully functioning churches in those days, there shouldn't have been much need of traveling revival preachers to come around and set up a tabernacle or some such spot and preach for several nights. But this one is said to have taken place, for at least one night, not very far from the Stricklin farm in Johnson County. They were great occasions, cutting down some of the loneliness and isolation of farm life, teaching folks about the Bible, and giving many people their first acquaintance with hymns. People would camp, mainly meaning sleep in their wagons, and enjoy meals prepared at the camp site with food everybody brought for the occasion. Families brought their kids, which is where Jack comes in.

Revival preachers were always reluctant to turn a captive audience loose, especially when they knew there were sure-enough sinners present who needed every possible chance of turning from their wicked ways, and this meeting was no different. Because they couldn't drive their wagons home in the dark, people had packed ahead of time for an early start the next day. And, so the story goes, the ones with babies had already tucked them in the backs of the wagons before heading over to hear the preaching, after which they said their goodbyes and went to bed. In the semi-darkness of the next morning, everybody with a baby checked to make sure the little ones were still tucked in and headed out for home. Only after the sun came up and the babies began to stir did people realize they all had the wrong babies! It was a scene of panic and chaos, as people began to figure out that someone had switched all the babies. With no way of getting in touch with anyone else, the only resolution was to go back to the campsite and hope everyone could get the babies straightened out. Decades after I was told this story, I heard a folklorist say that "switching the babies" is a migratory legend that appeared during the time of the camp meetings, a cautionary tale: "Be sure to check before you leave so you get home with the right baby!" After I reported on hearing this possible debunking of the baby-switching story, various family members began to wonder, did the story originate at a tent revival or camp meeting near Meeks's farm? Did it happen at all? Was it just a legend people told to warn parents to keep track of their babies? The reason it mattered to the Stricklin family was that everyone suspected Jack had been involved in the affair. In fact, in the last years of Meeks's life, Jack came to see him one time and confessed that he and some boys from a nearby farm had switched the babies. Meeks just said, "I always figured."

Alton himself figured in a little misbehavior on a historic occasion in the life of Grandview. He and one of the boys from a neighboring farm—he never would say if it was the same family as Uncle Jack's alleged accomplices in the baby-switching caper—managed to skip church one Sunday morning. That was bad enough, but they made it worse by going fishing. Alton loved to fish. It was something he tried to do as often as possible throughout his life. This time, he and his friend were fishing in a livestock pond, what Texans would call a "tank." It happened to be March 14, 1920, when Grandview's population was about fifteen hundred. Alton was twelve years old, old enough to have some pangs of conscience about fishing on Sunday morning. But that Sunday, a disastrous fire broke out in Grandview. No one was killed, but dozens of businesses and homes burned to the ground, churches too. Alton and his buddy didn't know the fire was happening, but they began talking about whether they were doing wrong and, if so, what the consequences might be. One of them mentioned the Devil and what might happen if they saw the old rascal coming for them. Just then, Alton's friend saw smoke coming up from behind Alton, toward the direction of Grandview, and said, "Well, looks like we won't have to wonder long. Yonder he comes!" Alton turned to look. When he turned back to say something to his friend, all he saw was the boy's fishing pole lying on the ground and the back of the other boy, who was running for his life.

In more ways than just having churches, Johnson County and the Antioch-Grandview-Cleburne area were well established by the last years of the nineteenth century, so the Stricklins weren't exactly pioneers. But life was still rugged, with all the work and the absence of comforts that went with farm life in the days before rural electrification and indoor plumbing. Alton's mother was Annie Lee Benton Stricklin, who had been one of Uncle Tom's students at the Antioch School. Her family, the Bentons, consisted of kindly men and formidable women and had some genuine claims to pioneer history. Annie's grandfather, Peter Stout Benton, had come to Johnson County in 1867 after having served as sheriff of Van Zandt County in East Texas, and her grandmother, Cynthia Ann Johnston, had come to Texas from Kentucky before the Civil War as a widow and the mother of several small children, traveling most of the way on flatboats. Alton's grandmother, Annie's mother, was Bettie Bascom Benton, and she ruled the family with an iron will. In spite of giving birth to seven children, she didn't think her offspring should have a bunch of kids themselves. She was sickly and, from all I could tell, extremely crabby. She died long before I was born, but family stories about her suggested she was something of a hypochondriac. She pretty much enslaved her daughter Lochie so she could take care of her, which kept Lochie from having much of a social life outside the family, let alone marrying.

One of the things that kept everyone going was music. Just about everybody in the Stricklin and Benton families sang or played some kind of musical instrument. The Bentons were very active Methodists and very involved in the musical activities of the church in Grandview. They were fascinated with funerals, for some reason, especially Annie's brother Will, who often would accompany the Grandview undertaker when he went out to someone's house to pick up a body. He always enjoyed telling the story of how his grandfather and father arrived in Grandview on June 1, 1867, the day of the funeral of an unidentified girl, presumably a murder victim, whose killing was one of the most notable events in the history of the town. Will played piano and organ at the Methodist church in Grandview. Annie showed an interest in the piano and took lessons and was a good singer. Before she married into the Church of Christ, she had been the organist at one of the area's Methodist churches, where her father was the song leader. Then, in 1910, she and Meeks saved up enough money to buy a piano for their oldest child and only daughter, Violet, who had had a terrible case of scarlet fever as a young girl and—because of the fever or the treatment she received—had some brain damage that left her unable to do many things as she grew up.

Medical care was certainly primitive in those days, and the Bentons and Stricklins were commonly at the mercy of whatever nostrums and remedies were provided by sometimes sparsely trained practitioners, such as what they called "rubbing doctors." But when Violet got old enough to sit on a piano bench, Annie and Will, who was very involved in the lives of his niece and nephews, showed her a few things on the keyboard and found out she had a lot of musical ability. Will and his twin brother, John, called Violet "Cicero" and were always very attentive to her. They also worked with the middle child, Benton, and he developed into a good musician. When Alton, who was nicknamed "Tot," got big enough, Uncle Will showed him some techniques on the piano, too, including the basics of ragtime music, which was very popular in those days. Uncle Will didn't have the sense of rhythm that Alton developed, but he would hop up and down on the piano bench when he played ragtime, something Alton picked up on when he played.

Before phonograph recordings and radio, especially out in the country, the main ways people learned music were either by ear, from someone who knew how to sing or play or both, or from sheet music, which formed a huge market in families across the United States. Uncle Will, like several of his siblings and in-laws, had studied music under traveling "masters" who would move into an area in those days and set up temporary "singing schools" and sometimes offer the basics of reading music and playing instruments, all of which was especially welcome among members and leaders of churches who couldn't afford to hire fulltime musicians to lead their worship services. The Church of Christ Stricklins, of course, didn't have that concern because of the prohibition in Churches of Christ against having instrumental music in worship. Learning to lead congregational singing could come in handy, but any uses of instruments to them were strictly for non-church music. The greatest outcome of musical life for the Stricklins, and in our family what was considered a striking coincidence, was that Alton's father was a breakdown fiddler, as were Bob Wills's father and, in time, Bob Wills himself.

Breakdown fiddling was a central feature of Texas fiddling traditions and—something that was terrifically important to Alton's later life—crucial to the ways Bob Wills's family embodied those traditions and, ultimately, the rise of western swing. Though "breakdown" was a term used by most people to refer to music for dances, also called hoedowns, in Meeks Stricklin's life it was mainly something for providing fun around the house and for use in fiddling contests that took place near enough to the farm in Johnson County that Meeks could get to them. He loved competing in those contests and went up against some of the greats of the day, including the legendary Alexander Campbell "Eck" Robertson, who in 1922 played the fiddle on what are considered the first recordings of country music. Meeks knew people could dance to the music he played, and he knew that there were families such as the Willses who provided music for square and round dancing in barns and houses all across the middle part of the United States. The fact that the members of the Church didn't approve of dancing didn't keep him from playing and enjoying the music. It just kept him from dancing. The contests he participated in were lively, entertaining affairs, featuring a lot of players who hammed it up, possibly knowing they needed to disguise the fact that they weren't necessarily great fiddlers. Once when he got back from a contest he hadn't won, someone asked if he'd been out-fiddled. He said, "No. I got out-danced." This doesn't mean that Meeks was a sourpuss. My sister Nancy, in fact, said that many times he would go outside and just holler out to no one in particular, just because it felt good to holler. And one of the things he really enjoyed was being around those other fiddlers and getting to listen to the music. He liked being part of that great tradition of country and small-town gatherings that grew into music festivals later. He passed that exuberance and love of playing music on to Alton.

Once he was about eight or so, old enough to sit by himself on the bench of his sister's piano, Alton told me in an interview in 1974, he "got up enough nerve to try to run up and down that keyboard a little bit." Armed with the knowledge of a few chords and the basics of rhythm, he began accompanying his father as Meeks played the fiddle. The old-timers called this "seconding." He learned to keep a steady beat, anticipate the chord changes, and stay out of the way of the melody the fiddle was creating, all crucial skills to have for people who play music by ear, that is, without the use of sheet music. He said, "We just played by the hour," especially at night, to "take the dreariness out a little bit. He'd saw around on the fiddle, and I'd beat around on that piano." Meeks loved to play "Taters in the Sandy Land," "Eighth of January," "Soldier's Joy," "Bonaparte's Retreat," and those sorts of tunes and would sing and holler while he played. But also, like countless American families with a piano in the parlor, the Stricklins had sheet music in the home. Because Alton's mother, Annie, sang and her brother Will played piano and organ, they had a great deal of sheet music for the popular tunes of the day. They sang and played around the house and in the homes of neighbors they visited. When some of the neighbors began to get phonograph machines, the Stricklins got to hear some of those songs at places they visited in and around Grandview.

In addition, several other family members knew how to play various instruments by ear. That's how Meeks played the fiddle, of course, and how Alton's sister, Violet, and Will's twin brother, John, played the guitar and mandolin. Long before he learned to read music, Alton played the piano by ear. One of the reasons I believe my father and Bob Wills hit it off was that they both grew up in families with fiddlers, and no one had to show Alton how to accompany Bob when the Texas Playboys headed into a fiddle tune. Seconding Bob could be challenging because of the ways he, like a lot of fiddlers, broke meter, that is, took liberties with the number of bars or measures through extending a note or a passage to give it more emphasis than would ordinarily appear in a song. In other words, the fiddler might hold a passage in a song longer than it normally would last before a chord change or change chords earlier than the song would typically provide for. Some people said "ear" musicians broke meter because they were unschooled and didn't know any better. I have always said you can't break meter if you don't know what it is, and Bob certainly knew what it was. Listen especially to the breakdowns and blues numbers he played, holding notes longer to add to the effect of the music. It drove some of the Texas Playboys crazy till they got the hang of accompanying Bob on these tunes, but to Alton, seconding a fiddler was the most natural thing he knew. In fact, he told me, "I never played much with anybody but my dad till I was grown, and I still use those things that I was working out when I was a kid playing with him, some of those old runs and licks I was hitting over fifty years ago."

His mother didn't think much of the jazz music Alton was getting increasingly interested in playing. The first jazzy song he ever played was "You Gotta See Your Mama Every Night (or You Can't See Her at All)," and Annie figured out that "your mama" didn't refer to anybody's sainted mother. Like a lot of people, she had the idea that jazz was only played "at wild places," but Alton's dad would wink at him and suggest quietly that it might be a good way to make a living. It turned out that Annie also had a cousin named Louis Chaney who played banjo around the time of World War I with the Original

Memphis Five, a pioneering jazz band. Alton said, "I got quite a lot of inspiration that I had this cousin who played for a while with the Memphis Five. He was one of my reasons for becoming interested in playing for a living."

Alton's first piano idol was Fletcher Harrison, the man who sold his parents the piano he learned to play on. Mr. Harrison tuned pianos and played very well, especially the ragtime tunes that appealed to Alton. He said, "I thought if I could ever learn to do that, I'd be the happiest person on earth." After he moved away from Grandview, Alton lost touch with Mr. Harrison, but in 1940, the Texas Playboys played a dance in San Angelo, Texas, at a place run by Mr. Harrison and his wife, who had moved out there and had a band called Harrison's Texans. He said,

> I hadn't seen him since I was a teenager when he'd come out and tune our piano. And we played that night, and he got up and introduced the band and said, "This young man that's playing the piano here, I sold his daddy the piano he learned to play on. He used to sit and watch me play. And I want to tell you, this boy is playing better than I ever thought I'd play. Now, I wish I could play like he does."

As he grew into a more confident piano player, Alton made the first money he ever earned from music, providing the accompaniment for a silent film playing at the movie house in Grandview. In those days in the big-city theaters, bands—in some cases they could have been considered orchestras—provided musical accompaniment for the action on screen in silent movies. In fact, many movies came with the sheet music the producers intended to be played during the picture. That wasn't the case in Grandview. One of Alton's friends from Grandview, a clarinetist named Bert Crouch, and a couple of other teenaged boys came out to the farm one summer day to ask Alton if he'd like to play with them at the theater in town. It was going to be a Tom Mix movie. They said they'd get three dollars apiece for the job. Alton told me that up till then he'd never made that much money in a year's time. When Alton asked Bert what he should play, he said, "We'll play fast songs when the horses are running and sad songs when someone's dying and waltzes during the love scenes." Alton told Bert, "You'll have to ask my mother." Annie said yes, and the boys had a great time, playing "Tiger Rag" and the "Washington and Lee Swing" and "On, Wisconsin." Alton didn't know all the songs they played, but because he had a good ear, he could follow along. Good experience for a musician who might end up playing in a dance band someday. He got more musical training while in high school in Grandview, especially in the town band, led by Otis Hale, who taught Alton and brother Benton to play an alto-pitched brass instrument often referred to as a "peck horn." Their Uncle Will played clarinet in that band.

In the summer of 1926, two friends who knew Benton at Thorp Spring Christian College got in touch with Alton about going with them on a trip to the Rio Grande Valley. One was Ezra Dodson, a drummer and dancer who wanted to start an orchestra in the Valley and call it the Rio Grande Serenaders. The other guy was Manley Head, who became Alton's dear, lifelong friend and who attended the Asleep at the Wheel show in 1974. Ezra needed a piano player and wanted Alton to go with them. He and Manley came by the farm to talk him into going. Alton was just eighteen years old and had never played in an actual band, other than that one night at the movie theater in Grandview. Ezra's family lived in San Benito, and they had a ride lined up to get as far south as Georgetown. The plan was to hitchhike from there and try to entertain people in restaurants and so on to get some free meals. They got a room in the Hotel Pershing in Austin for twenty-five cents but couldn't sleep because of the heat, so they checked out and walked to the edge of town and slept in the furrows of a cotton field. They looked for eating places with pianos. Alton would play. Ezra would sing and dance. Manley would go around collecting nickels and dimes from the customers. After a couple of days, they made it to San Benito, and Ezra started putting the orchestra together. For money, Alton also worked part-time in Ezra's father's grocery store. They played some dances and then got a job at a theater in Pharr, playing for stage shows—magicians, jugglers, and the like. By the end of the summer, Alton needed to get back for his last year of high school and hitchhiked back to Grandview. A couple of years later, he did much the same thing to play briefly with the Jean Goldkette Orchestra in San Antonio, filling in for their regular piano player, who was recovering from an injury.

High school offered Alton various kinds of opportunities, including the chance to play sports. He had played basketball at the rural Johnson County Rock Tank School, and he and Benton played basketball and football with the Grandview Zebras. Alton recalled a trip to play a game in the town of West, Texas, which has a strong Czech community and now enjoys a reputation as a fun place to visit, especially to pick up Czech pastries. In those days, though, Alton said they weren't very welcoming to visiting football teams. He called the people of West "Bohemians," using an old name for Czechs, and talked about how they played football on a field full of stinging nettle, which the tough local boys were used to but which bothered the visitors a lot. People don't often associate musicians with sports, but Alton's love of athletics was a big part of who he was. In addition to playing football and basketball, he became quite a track star in high school. Later in life, as he gained quite a bit of weight, people had a hard time imagining him as a sprinter, but a sprinter he was, and quite a good one. Alton broke ten seconds in the hundred-yard dash *in the 1920s*, which was blazing for a high school kid in those days and was considered very fast for quite a while thereafter. Alton had a bit of bad luck, though, after qualifying for the regional track meet in high school. He didn't have a way to get to the meet, which took place in Dallas. It was about fifty miles from Grandview, and neither the school nor his family could help him get there. He hitchhiked to the outskirts of Dallas, caught a streetcar, and walked into the stadium in his street clothes as they were making the last call for his heat of the hundred-yard dash. He hurriedly stripped to his running shorts and shirt, dug his starting holes in those days before starting blocks, and ran the race with no more warm-up than running to the starting line after hearing the last call. Unsurprisingly, he didn't do very well. But running track helped him get a toehold in the world of college.

It was certainly not automatic that Alton and his brother would go to college. The family didn't have much money to spare, but the boys were encouraged to "make something" of themselves. And they believed they were well prepared to do college work. The rural schools in Rock Tank and Antioch, like so many schools of the day, were organized around a curriculum that stressed the three Rs but also vast amounts of memorization, particularly of poetry, something Alton reveled in. That was accelerated when he got to Grandview High School, which was in many ways rooted in the classical philosophy of education, exemplified by the concentration on learning poetry and on speaking with proper diction. It had an effect on him. In fact, for the rest of his life, he had a public speaking style that was different from his regular voice. Also, throughout his life, he was apt to launch into a recitation of poems he had learned as a kid, such as

William Cullen Bryant's mournful "Thanatopsis" and George Pope Morris's lighter-hearted "Woodman, Spare That Tree," stopping as he walked through a room and regaling the sometimes-startled listeners with verse. Family photos show that Alton, Benton, and Violet dressed nicely and stayed well groomed. There was always an understanding that Violet's limitations would keep her close to home. The boys helped with the farming but never seemed to consider that as a way of making a living. They both took part in what was called then "comprehensive military training," which amounted to a less dramatic version of the basic training actual enlistees in the military services experienced. Alton's main recollection from those days was that the instructor was friendly toward everyone in the unit and called Alton "A-cut" and Benton "B-cut."

Their Uncle Will, the church organist, had been drafted into the Army during World War I and made it to France. He had little interest in hunting and other outdoor pursuits and didn't want to go to war. His twin brother, John, who was more of an outdoors-type person, wanted to go but couldn't because of his bad eyesight. Will was spared the horrors of trench warfare, though. The Armistice was signed about two weeks before his unit was scheduled to go up to the front. Because of military censorship, the letters and cards he sent home from France were lacking in specific information about where he was and what his unit was doing. He mostly inquired about how people in Grandview were doing in the face of the terrible influenza pandemic, which killed millions worldwide and dozens in his small hometown. But he did include in one of his letters home a long description of how happy he was to find a workable organ in an abandoned French church he ventured into. He said that playing that organ was the highlight of his entire time in the service. He and his company came back to the United States, took a photo in a field on

Long Island, and mustered out. He came back to Texas on the train and, as far as I know, never again traveled more than a hundred miles from the spot of his birth on the Benton farm. Alton and Benton didn't want to go off to war someday, but they did figure on getting out into a larger world than they knew on the farm. They expected that a key move toward that goal for kids who had been good students in high school involved going to college.

Alton and Benton were in the field chopping cotton in the summer of 1927 when the dean of Weatherford College drove up and asked to speak with them. He'd been visiting in Grandview, and someone told him there were these Stricklin brothers who were nice young men and musicians and athletes. The dean told them he'd give them scholarships to cover their tuition if they would participate in college musical groups and sports teams at Weatherford. They visited the campus, took a liking to it, and started school that fall. They both played in the band and sang in the glee club. Alton played piano in the college orchestra, which Benton directed and which went on some promotional tours for the college. They picked up odd jobs to cover room and board and shared a house with four other sets of Weatherford College brothers. Then, in 1928, Alton got a full scholarship to attend the short-lived Thorp Spring Christian College, which moved to Terrell that fall and changed its name to Texas Christian College (not to be confused with Texas Christian University, the Disciples of Christ school that had been in Thorp Spring briefly but was now in Fort Worth). Benton had attended the Church of Christ–affiliated school when it was at the Thorp Spring campus near Granbury. Alton played in their band, ran track, and coached the track team. He thought it was odd to be the coach of a team he was a member of, but practices were informal at small schools in those days, so that's what he did. In the band, Alton played a peck horn he had bought in

Terrell for three dollars and got Mr. Hale in Grandview to give him some more lessons on it. He was glad to strengthen his music-reading ability but knew his musical future didn't reside in brass instruments. It was, most certainly, in playing the piano.

CHAPTER 3

Baylor

After finishing the 1928–29 school year at Terrell, Alton went to see an old Grandview buddy, Barney Hale, in Waco. Barney had made a name for himself as a football player on the Grandview Zebras squad and had gotten a spot on the team at Baylor. He was also the son of the leader of the Grandview town band who had taught Alton and Benton to play the peck horn. Knowing Alton's talent and growing reputation as a musician, Barney asked Alton if he wanted to watch the football team work out and, after that was over, play some music for the team. After the workout, players and coaches alike moved to a room with a piano, and Alton went to work on some jazz tunes. After playing for about a half hour, he was approached by one of Baylor's star players, Jake Wilson, who was about to start a season that saw him win All-Southwest Conference honors. Jake asked Alton what he was planning to do in the fall. Alton said he didn't know and didn't think he'd be able to do any more college work because the money just wasn't there. This was before the infamous stock market crash in the fall of 1929, but he told me in an interview that, "Within a few months, the only people who could go to school were those who could work or whose parents were rich." Alton's parents certainly weren't rich, and jobs were hard to come by. Jake wouldn't hear of it and told Alton to think about coming to Baylor anyway. He said, "A man that can play the piano like you can doesn't need money." Alton went back to the farm and, a few days later, the phone rang. It was Jake Wilson, calling from Grandview, asking if he was ready to go. He hadn't even told his parents about the conversations or anything about prospects for going to Baylor. It was just too hard to imagine, and not because Baptist-related Baylor was famously straightlaced. It mainly had to do with the lack of money for school and what seemed to Alton like lousy timing. Jake wouldn't have it. He said he was heading out to the farm and would pick him up. Ten minutes later, Alton was packing. They loaded up and headed for Waco. On the trip down, Jake outlined his plan for getting Alton enrolled at Baylor.

When they got to the campus, he took Alton to see the Baylor cashier and asked for what amounted to a line of credit toward the fall term's tuition. The cashier said they didn't do things that way. This was long before student loans became a common way of financing college, and extending credit for school expenses was a good way for a university to go out of business. But Jake Wilson was a major campus celebrity, a genuine football hero, and a supremely self-confident young man. He told the cashier that Alton's daddy up in Johnson County was about to sell a "bunch of cattle" and that Jake would guarantee Alton would pay his tuition bill before the end of the term. Besides, he said, "We need this guy down here. He's a great musician. He can put life into a college." Giving in to the persuasive football star, the cashier agreed to the plan and gave Alton six weeks to pay up. As they walked out of his office, Alton told Jake, "My daddy doesn't own a 'bunch of cattle.' All he has is one old milk cow!" Jake said not to worry about it, that it would all work out.

Jake kept at his project of getting Alton established at Baylor. He introduced Alton to Rollin Monroe, a bass player who had a band that needed a piano player. Alton started picking up some money playing some dances, though strictly off campus. Dancing was banned at Baylor in those days and for decades afterward. Then Jake told him he and Barney had arranged for him to play the piano at an upcoming pep rally. After Alton had played a couple of numbers, Jake called out to the crowd, "How many of you would like to be able to play the piano like that?" Dozens raised their hands, and Jake announced that Alton would be happy to talk to any of them about giving lessons. Alton was, of course, astonished to find out he was about to become a piano teacher but happy to get a line on another source of income. Jake also arranged for a piano to be set up in the university dining hall and for Alton to get free meals for playing for the other students. Barney solved the problem of a place to sleep when he suggested that Alton could sleep on the floor in Barney's dormitory room until he could get a place of his own. So he "stole a room," as he used to tell it, for a term. With the money he made playing with local bands, playing at the dining hall at Baylor, and giving piano lessons, he met the six-week deadline to pay his tuition. And he earned a half-credit for playing in the Baylor band, though he had to drop out when the bandleader wouldn't let him march with his beat-up old peck horn. He didn't have the money to buy a new one. By the end of his first term at Baylor, he was able to get off the floor of Barney Hale's room in Brooks Hall and move into a boarding house, much to his relief. He had hated the idea of not paying for a room on campus and stayed nervous that he and Barney would get caught and kicked out of school. That very fate awaited Alton, but for different reasons.

When he arrived at Baylor, Alton knew exactly two people in Waco, Barney Hale and Jake Wilson, but Barney and Jake were good ones to know. They got Alton connected with campus life at what was then a very small school but one with notions about making an impact on civic and religious life in Texas. Baylor had been chartered in 1845 in one of the last acts of the Republic of Texas, before Texas became one of the United States, and the university had been through some rough times. Alton got there in the fall of 1929, just as the economic downturn in the United States and other countries was getting very serious. But there was a lively spirit at the place, prompted to a great degree by Baylor's membership in the Southwest Conference. Having rivalries with the big state schools—Arkansas, Texas, and Texas A&M (this was before the addition of Texas Tech)—and the other private schools—Rice, SMU, and TCU—created a lot of excitement, especially during football season. Because of his connections to members of the football team and the invitation to play at a pep rally in his first fall at Baylor, he quickly became known around campus and picked up the nickname "Strick."

In those days, Baylor occupied a much smaller spot on Waco's South Fifth Street than it does today. Barney Hale's room in Brooks Hall, with his secret roommate from Grandview, was on the edge of the campus that runs alongside Interstate Highway 35 today. Most classes were held in the original buildings on the Burleson Quadrangle, which included the Carroll Library and Carroll Science Building, along with Burleson Hall, which housed a dormitory for women. A favorite pastime of Baylor boys was to climb the fire escape on the side of Carroll Library and try to peer through the windows of Burleson Hall and see the young women getting ready for bed. My father confessed that he had engaged in this activity on several occasions. He also became friends with one of his history instructors, a young man named Raymond Dillard. They ran around together at night pretty often, and after one such late outing, Alton was having trouble staying awake. Young Professor Dillard interrupted his lecture and said, "Mr. Stricklin, if you'd get some sleep at night, you might be better able to stay awake in my class!" His history instructors made a particular impression on him, especially longtime department chair Francis Guittard and legendary character Guy B. Harrison. Professor Harrison was one of those unpredictable, highly theatrical lecturers who loved catching students off guard, most famously when he climbed through the window of his third-floor classroom, from one of those handy fire escapes, to give a pop quiz after having previously told the class, "Why, I'd no sooner climb through that window than ever give you a pop quiz." One of Alton's political science professors—remember, this was the late 1920s—once told a class Alton was in, "Students, I want to tell you about a new leader in Europe who is really making strides with his country, someone who will be regarded as one of the true architects of the twentieth century." And then he wrote the leader's name on the blackboard so everyone could copy it down: Benito Mussolini. I'm sure everyone in that class wished they could have talked to that professor ten years later to find out what he thought then about the Italian fascist. Alton was very fond of his Spanish professor, Andres Sendon, and took enough courses to become a fairly good Spanish speaker. He got a Spanish pen pal, a young woman, through Professor Sendon and gave a good bit of thought to trying to visit Spain to meet her, thinking a romance might develop. There was also talk about becoming a foreign-exchange teacher. The expense of the trip made it highly unlikely, of course, but he always said he wondered what would have happened if he could have gone over there.

Alton became well-known because of his unusual approach to piano lessons, what he called the "short method." A growing number of students were hearing him play around campus and around Waco, and a lot of them thought they'd like to have as much fun playing the piano as Strick seemed to be having. Of course, many of them had had formal piano lessons, often with grim teachers who howled to the heavens if one of their students departed in the least from what appeared on the sheet music. This was what set Alton apart from other piano players and showed why he never called himself a "pianist." His students who caught on to his method for having fun with the piano had to have a good ear. If all they could play was what was written on the sheet, he couldn't do much with them, much to the relief of their elders and, if they got wind of any of this, their old piano teachers! Word got around that there was this fellow corrupting the young pianists of Waco, and Alton was made aware that his short method was frowned upon. But his students probably had some fun with it, getting to where they could play a melody by ear and know how to use chord patterns and some structural elements musicians in bands used.

One such technique was known as the "turn-around," which was a series of chords (for instance, in the key of C: C, C sharp, D, and G) band members could repeat while a vocalist was coming to the microphone or something else was happening that needed a little extra time, a maneuver also known as "vamping." There was also "going around the bend," which was another series of chords (for instance, again in the key of C: F, F minor, C, A, D, G, C) that often marked the transition to another verse. Alton would demonstrate these little methods with popular tunes from the 1920s and '30s, showing how they had a lot of elements in common. One time, to show me how often similar chord changes and other features showed up in different songs, he played "Five Foot Two," "Please Don't Talk about Me When I'm Gone," and "Darkness on the Delta" and said, "Listen to that. It's all basically the same song!"

It was the Jazz Age, but Alton didn't expect students to learn to improvise the way he did, which was inspired by the jazz music he was hearing. But he did want his students to be able to play with the joy and sense of abandon he always felt and which he thought they could experience if they could learn to use syncopation. This aspect of music was something he learned at a very early age from his family, especially his Uncle Will, the Methodist church organist and piano player at the Grandview church. Playing instrumental music in church was a skill that had no value for the Church of Christ Stricklins, of course, but Will's knowledge of ragtime music was like pure gold itself to Alton. Ragtime is built on syncopation, and syncopation wasn't something many classically trained musicians of the period thought proper.

•••

Campus life at Baylor in the 1920s and '30s was intimate. The student body was small, and most of the students knew each other. One sad outgrowth of that was the still-raw memory of the tragic deaths of ten Baylor students in January 1927 at Round Rock. The basketball team was on the way to Austin to play the University of Texas. In wretched weather at a poorly marked railroad crossing, the Baylor team bus was hit by a train. A team member named Clyde "Abe" Kelley pushed a smaller student, his roommate, through one of the windows of the bus just before the train smashed into it, saving his life. Alton knew one of the surviving students and said he didn't think he ever knew anyone sadder. Another of the survivors of the Round Rock train collision was John "Killer" Kane, who became one of Baylor's most highly decorated military figures, receiving the Medal of Honor during World War II for leading a breathtakingly dangerous 1943 airstrike on Romanian oil refineries under Nazi control.

One happy outgrowth of the fact that most students knew each other was that Alton earned a reputation for having a quick wit. On a chilly winter morning, he was coming down the steps of one of the campus buildings, Old Main, which had some icy buildup and were slippery. He was stepping very carefully when suddenly he felt a tug on his arm. A female student next to him had lost her footing and pulled Alton down on his rear end, whereupon she landed in his lap, and they proceeded to bump, bump, bump down the remaining steps until they came to rest on the sidewalk of the Burleson Quadrangle. It was a miracle neither of them broke any bones, but what most people probably remembered about the incident was the announcement Alton made when he and his companion landed on the sidewalk: "You can get off now, Anna Laura. This is as far as I go."

Alton recalled the occasional feelings of awe often experienced by college students who are away from home, having to study, and being exposed to the great ideas of the age. But he also recalled the cutting-up and carrying-on of college students, even at Baptist Baylor. What was known for many years as Burleson Quadrangle featured a very formal statue of former President Rufus C. Burleson, depicting him in all his gathered dignity. Unfortunately, the statue featured an outstretched top hat, as those were still popular in Burleson's day. Despite the fact that Prohibition was still the law of the land in the late 1920s, and despite the strict anti-booze teachings of Baptists, a common Saturday night occurrence in those days was the appearance of several empty beer bottles in President Burleson's top hat. The bottles were numerous enough to stick up out of the hat, in full view of anyone going down Fifth Street on their way to church on Sunday morning. My father never came right out and said he had been one of the bottle depositors, but he did express some admiration for the culprits. The prank was repeated so often that someone in the university administration finally directed the school's groundskeepers to fill the hat with cement.

Alton always loved sports and really enjoyed going to Baylor athletic events. One of his favorite forms of entertainment was to go to baseball games and hear the salty language of the Baylor catcher, Barton "Botchey" Koch (pronounced "cook"). Koch was a stalwart on the football team as well, the Southwest Conference's first All-American. The trash talk that Koch and other players used was easier to hear at a baseball game than it was on a football field, and one of the more delicate professors, a baseball fan but not a fan of bad language, would admonish him during the game, saying, "Watch your language, Barton. Children and ladies are present." Botchey apparently thought his language was plenty appropriate, given the rough-and-tumble action at home plate he was often involved in.

Alton was a member of the Baylor track team. His running times were good on the junior-college level, but he wasn't quite up to the standards of the Southwest Conference of those days. His claim to a funny sort of track fame came one day when the famous Finnish distance runner Paavo Nurmi came to town. Nurmi had won eleven gold and silver medals in Olympic competition in the 1920s and held the world record for the mile run at the time of his visit to Baylor. He was barnstorming around the United States, running exhibition races at track meets for publicity and prize money, and he offered to run a mile against a relay team of four Baylor runners. Of course, even the famous "Flying Finn" would have had a hard time beating Baylor's best mile-relay team, so the Baylor coach offered the backup team made up of sprinters, not quarter milers, to give Nurmi a sporting chance. Alton was one of those runners and, like a lot of sprinters and like the other three fellows on the mile-relay B-team, could do well for about three hundred yards. Sprinters talk about "hitting the wall" just as they turn onto the straightaway to the finish line, which is exactly what happened to Alton and his teammates, four times.

Each Baylor runner would go zooming off to a big lead over Nurmi, who kept his pace and glided his way past each sprinter on the final stretch in plenty of time to win each lap and, finally, the race. It was a great crowd pleaser, if a little embarrassing for the four Baylor boys. Still, they got to shake hands with one of the greatest athletes of the twentieth century.

Other aspects of life at Baylor were a little frustrating. Having grown up in a family that went to church and having scads of relatives who were active in church, sacred music, even preaching, Alton was comfortable with churchly language and expectations. But Baylor's Baptist origins and connections had an outsized influence on the culture at the school. No one ever claimed that Baylor was a "Bible college," a dismissive term for a school with a narrow curriculum intended to give its students what in some ways amounted to a post-graduate course in Sunday school and send them out to teach or preach or both in one or more of the thousands of evangelical congregations scattered about the United States. Because of the way Baptist congregations ordained ministers, without any absolute requirement of seminary training or, really, any education of any kind, a lot of people attended churches in Texas and elsewhere led by poorly equipped ministers. There were brilliant exceptions, of course, including many Baylor graduates who distinguished themselves in advanced studies in theology and ministry and could have contributed admirably to the life of any congregation, university, or seminary. And, as the twentieth century went on, Texas Baptists and other Baptists in the South included advocates of extending the full benefits of U.S. citizenship to African Americans, peace activists, and proponents of women's rights, even those who favored the ordination of women to the ministry, which was unthinkable for many Baptists in the first half of the century. But, in the late 1920s, there were widespread forces among

Baptists and other evangelicals trying to put the genie of modernism back in its bottle and return the United States to some rosy past they thought had existed when churches ruled everybody's behavior and nobody's mind was confused by science.

It also was a time when most Baptists and Catholics held deep suspicions toward one another. Baptists, with their congregational form of governance, viewed the hierarchy of the Roman Catholic Church, the sacramental system that guided the behavior of Catholics at every stage of life, and the vast authority of the pope with deep distrust. To a great extent, that low regard only began to trail off when Catholic John F. Kennedy got elected to the presidency in 1960. When Alton was at Baylor in the late 1920s, anti-Catholic hysteria was a big part of the regular diet of the evangelical world and especially of its hardest core, the fundamentalists who wanted to take over Protestant churches and organizations and impose their beliefs on everyone else. This contingent was chastened a little by the embarrassing episode from 1925 in Dayton, Tennessee, when a public high school teacher was convicted of teaching the theory of evolution, and national media figures portrayed the anti-evolution crowd as flat-earth primitives. But the forces of fundamentalism were strong, determined, and ruthless. Any religiously affiliated school had to be ready to defend itself against charges of loose morals and scandalous misbehavior.

One of the ways Baylor defended itself against those charges was through an informal body of informants who would tattle on fellow students they saw drinking or carrying on in other ways. It was never clear whether the university had actually recruited these spies to police the morals of their fellow students, but their activities helped ward off critics who were eager to condemn Baylor for being too lax, too "modern." The snitches tended to be what their victims called "preacher boys," young men who were only undergraduates but who were already serving as pastors of churches, mostly in small towns near enough to the university that they could get back and forth between the campus and their congregations. Because just about any male with a decent reputation could find a congregation somewhere to ordain him, it was not terribly unusual to find a church with a pastor barely out of his teen years, possibly still in them. Alton had a very strong reason to believe one of those preacher boys got him kicked out of Baylor.

Soon after arriving in Waco, as he was getting better and better known for his piano playing, Alton got in with other musicians around town. Word always travels fast among musicians when somebody comes along who really has some talent, and band members are always trying to figure out combinations of instruments and personalities to make their music more interesting and, just maybe, profitable. Alton played with several bands during his time in Waco, and, like most small groups of players, those bands played a lot of dances. Sometimes they would play at pavilions in parks, which made it hard to get paid. If people could sit in their cars and hear the music, to save the quarter or so it cost to get onto the dance floor they sometimes just stayed back and sat in their cars. Alton and his bandmates were so desperate one time to get people to buy a ticket and get into the actual dance that every time a car drove up, the band leader would say, "Here comes one, boys. Hit 'Dinah,'" a popular dance tune they were sure would get people out of their cars. A better way was to hold a dance in an enclosed structure with a ticket seller at the door, which was exactly the set-up at the dance that got Alton into trouble.

It was Waco's Knights of Columbus Hall, a venue run by the Catholic men's organization. Alton and some other guys played there twice a week, on Wednesday and Saturday nights, and made eight dollars apiece, which wasn't a bad paycheck in those days. After the dance one Saturday night, Alton was summoned to the president's office. When he got there, he was met by Dr. S. P. Brooks himself, the imposing president of the university. Alton and the other band members who were Baylor students were told that university officials had reason to believe they had played in a band at a public dance at the K.C. Hall and that, even worse, liquor was consumed on the premises. The boys admitted that they had played the dance but denied drinking any alcohol. Drinking was not only immoral, from Dr. Brooks's perspective, but also illegal. The boys said they were just trying to make enough money to stay in school and hadn't done anything bad. Not persuaded of their innocence, Dr. Brooks informed them that they were no longer students at Baylor. Alton and his mates went to see Dean W. Sims Allen, who told them they could be reinstated after a while if they kept out of trouble. Alton, of course, didn't bring up the fact that he had previously "stolen" a term's worth of lodging in Brooks Hall, which was named for the formidable Baylor president, but he thought there might be a file on him that held that information and put him on even thinner ice with the university. He didn't know then what he might have learned later: that Dr. Brooks was under immense pressure to keep Baylor free of the kinds of scandals, small and large, that the university's fundamentalist critics hoped to use to run down the school; also that Brooks was a strong defender of academic freedom, warding off attempts to get Baylor to offer anti-evolutionist notions in place of scientific findings in biology and geology courses. Nevertheless, Alton had a very strong impression that his fate at Baylor was sealed by one of the preacher boys. How a fellow who wasn't at the dance knew what was going on inside the K.C. Hall, Alton never found out. It wasn't very likely that one of those guys was willing to risk being close to so many sinners! He also was never sure whether it was playing a public dance that got him kicked out or if it was playing at a venue run by a Catholic organization. He figured it was probably a little of both.

Alton hadn't gone to college with a clear career plan. Like many first-generation college students, he came from a family that didn't know much about how universities worked. Alton's Uncle John had wanted to go to college. He would have been the first member of the family to do so, but he decided to stay put when his father offered to give him some acreage to start his own farm. He worked that land until he was killed on it in a farm accident at the age of eighty-one. The Stricklins and Bentons were readers. They paid attention to world affairs—Alton remembered listening to Hitler on a shortwave radio at a neighboring family's home. He said they couldn't understand what he was saying, of course, but they found his anger remarkable. The family valued education and encouraged Alton and his brother to get as much of it as they could. They even arranged for Alton to live with a family in Grandview while he was finishing high school to make it easier to keep up with his studies. They just didn't know much about what someone would do with a college education. Although President Brooks had instituted several aspects of student services at Baylor that were in the process of becoming standard features of modern universities, most schools didn't offer much in the way of academic or career counseling in those days, so it wasn't as if getting kicked out of school derailed some grand plan Alton had. He just didn't know what to do next. He had some interest in teaching. He even thought some more about trying to get to Spain.

Instead, he went back to Baylor briefly, got reinstated, and tried to make a go of it. But he'd been thrown off balance somewhat by getting kicked out, and by then the Great Depression was ravaging everything. He was just flat broke. He went to see Dean Allen and told him he was going to take a couple of quarters off and see if he could build up some cash and come back. The kindly dean remembered him from the unfortunate K.C. Hall episode and tried to talk him into staying in school, saying, "If you leave now, you'll never come back." And that's exactly what happened. Whatever he might have done with a college degree, he was now almost totally assured of never getting one. The Depression added one more college dropout to its statistical price tag of disruption and upheaval.

Alton always regretted not getting a Baylor diploma. Despite the unhappy experience of getting kicked out of school, he always loved Baylor and especially appreciated Dean Allen's kindness. He wasn't that crazy about the more forbidding President Brooks, though he always referred to Dr. Brooks as "a wonderful man and a great educator." And he was grateful to have been readmitted as a student. He found some irony in the fact that Dr. Brooks's last term at Baylor, the spring of 1931, would have been his last one at Baylor, if he could have kept going with his schoolwork. In one of those stories that colleges and universities love to tell about legendary characters, it so happened that Dr. Brooks was dying as that term came to an end. He had been signing diplomas for the upcoming graduation ceremonies, but his strength gave out somewhere in the middle of the alphabet, and he was unable to sign diplomas for the entire class. I always wondered what Dr. Brooks would have thought if he had had the opportunity to sign my father's diploma, if he would have remembered the name of the kid he kicked out of school. But he ran out of strength before he got to the students whose last names started with S. So, he wouldn't have been able to sign it, even if there had been a diploma to sign. Years later, leading up to the celebration of Baylor's one-hundred-fiftieth anniversary, the Baylor Alumni Association magazine included Alton in a set of profiles of one hundred fifty notable former students, along with John "Killer" Kane, people who had made a mark "upon the world through their exceptional achievements." The piece doesn't say he got kicked out of Baylor, but it does mention playing at the Knights of Columbus Hall, which it says he did once a week, with a group called the Unholy Three.

That wasn't quite right. He played there twice a week and with a different band, but the alumni association's profile highlighted an interesting set of ironies. The reason Alton was included in the list of notable former students was the fame he had gained playing with Bob Wills, which he wouldn't have had if he had stayed at Baylor, gotten his degree, and gone to work doing whatever he could have found to do with a college diploma. If he'd done all that, he might have become well known for some other reason, but it wouldn't have been because he'd been one of the original Texas Playboys. He got kicked out of school for doing what ended up making him "notable," and it was probably the best thing that ever happened to him professionally. Instead of trying to plug away at getting a degree, he planned to head up to Fort Worth and try to get a foothold in the music business. He didn't know then that Bob Wills was in Fort Worth doing the very same thing.

Al at the age of three.

Zebedee Meeks and Annie Lee Benton Stricklin, Al's parents.

Al as a baby in his mother's arms; musician uncles on the right.

Al's Uncle Will Benton's "singing school" diploma for proficiency in organ and piano.

INTERNATIONAL CONSERVATORY OF MUSIC.
DALLAS, TEXAS.

Be it Known To all to whom these presents come

That G. Will Benton

Having honorably completed the first year's course of study on the Organ

under the instruction of the

International Conservatory of Music

Is entitled to this

CERTIFICATE.

Dated at Dallas, Texas, this the Twenty first day of August A.D. 1908

Al's Uncle Will in his World War I Army uniform. Will taught him the rudiments of piano playing.

Will *(left)* and his twin brother, John, with musician cousins.

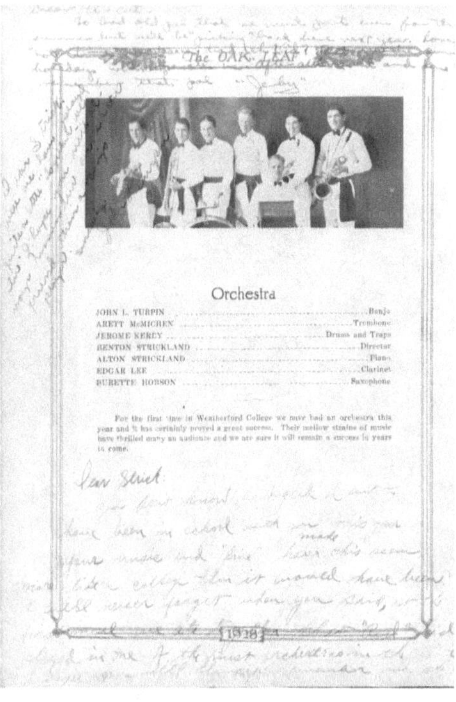

The OAK LEAF

Orchestra

JOHN L. TURPIN .... Banjo
ARETT McMICHEN .... Trombone
JEROME KEREY .... Drums and Traps
BENTON STRICKLAND .... Director
ALTON STRICKLAND .... Piano
EDGAR LEE .... Clarinet
BURETTE HOBSON .... Saxophone

For the first time in Weatherford College we have had an orchestra this year and it has certainly proved a great success. Their mellow strains of music have thrilled many an audience and we are sure it will remain a success in years to come.

1928

Al *(seated)* with Benton *(standing, third from right)* in the Weatherford College Orchestra in 1928, last name misspelled.

Al *(right)* with Benton while they were college students.

Al *(right)* next to his brother, Benton, as teenagers.

Al *(third from left)* with relatives, including his sister Violet *(second from right)*, whose piano he learned to play on.

Al's mother, Annie, with her sisters, Lochie, Cora, and Bertie *(left to right)*.

Al, Larry White, and Doug Blair *(right to left)* as the Tune Tinkers on KFJZ in Fort Worth.

CHAPTER 4

Tune Tinker

Alton loved telling the story of how he met Bob Wills. After they both had been knocked around a bit and had some eye-opening experiences in life and in music, they met, appropriately, at a radio station. Bob had come to Fort Worth in 1929, having grown up in Limestone County and then Hall County in a family of farmers and fiddlers. He learned to play music from his family and sharpened his skills in the barn dances and house dances that were such an important form of entertainment for people who lived and worked hard in rural areas and small towns and needed to kick up their heels every now and then and have some fun. Bob had also played music and done comedy routines on medicine shows. These were old-fashioned live acts meant to gather crowds in vacant lots and city parks so a fast-talking pitch artist on the back of a wagon or a flatbed truck could sell what they called "patent medicines," also known as "snake oil," weird concoctions pitched as cures for just about anything from ingrown toenails to "female troubles" to thinning hair. It was a form of performance that quickened the wits and probably served Bob well as he moved from thinking of himself as a house-dance fiddler to thinking he could be a full-fledged bandleader. When he started making records with the Texas Playboys, he would occasionally come out with lines from comedy routines and songs he had learned in the medicine shows, and those experiences stuck with him in other ways. As Alton told it, Bob and guitarist Herman Arnspiger and vocalist Milton Brown came into the studio at KFJZ in Fort Worth to try to get on the radio, which was the dream of lots of people who wanted to try to make a living playing music.

It's hard to imagine today how totally dominant radio was in the American entertainment landscape in the early 1930s. The record industry was becoming very important, as were movies. But you had to have money to buy records or go to a movie. If you could get a radio or make friends with somebody who had one, you had free entertainment forever. Radios could be expensive. At first, only people in middle-class families were able to buy radios, which in those days often meant a bunch of glass tubes inside a wooden case the size of a small refrigerator, three or four feet high. They were usually sold in furniture stores. You'd turn the thing on, wait several seconds for it to warm up—which meant waiting for these mysterious tubes to start to glow—turn a knob that controlled the frequency dial, and find the station you wanted to listen to. Despite the initial cost of becoming a radio owner, by the late 1920s, increasing numbers of people had bought one. And a vast segment of the United States was within the broadcast radius of at least one radio station, often lots of them as local entrepreneurs figured out the technology, organized ways to get sponsors to pay for advertising, and started broadcasting. Most stations were only on the air for part of the day. They might broadcast into the evening and then "sign off" until the next morning. But no matter how much airtime they needed to fill, there was a huge demand for material to send out to listeners. That ranged everywhere from sermons by local preachers to poems read aloud by teachers and little inspirational talks meant to get people's minds on higher purposes than the usual misbehavior and degradation they might get up to if left to themselves. Much of this was set to a wide variety of music, the vast majority of it played and sung live in the studio of the broadcasting station.

When these local radio stations went on the air, nearly all of them had program managers who decided what would go out and when. Blocks of time devoted to a particular kind of music or a locally popular musician might be as brief as fifteen minutes. Sometimes, sponsorships could be sold more easily for short segments, which helped local businesses get the word out about their wonderful products and services. But the radio station's program manager had a real chore finding the talent needed to fill all those programming slots. Once national networks started sending programs out, stations in larger towns such as Dallas and Fort Worth got several hours a day of programming from the network they could just put on the air and not have to worry about. That put all kinds of music and other forms of creative material within reach of people who had never heard anything like it, let alone tried to perform it themselves. But it still meant that most stations had to fill time, even those affiliated with the networks. There's no telling how many amateur musicians played for radio stations, taking time off from their jobs or their farming, hoping to catch on and become famous and rich or just hoping to have a little fun and a few moments of local celebrity. Some, of course, did catch on and became famous. That's what happened with Bob Wills and his bandmates.

Alton was the staff piano player at KFJZ in 1931, along with being the collector of unpaid bills, which he said was a job he didn't do very well. He had been working there off and on since leaving Baylor and playing with various dance bands in the Fort Worth area.

Most days, being a staff musician at a radio station meant that he and a couple of other guys would play a fifteen-minute or half-hour show in one style and then come back later, throw in a different instrument or trade being the lead vocalist, and call themselves something else. The fellows he played with most often were Doug Blair and Larry White. Doug played saxophone and clarinet, and Larry played banjo, guitar, and ukulele. They all sang. Alton had met them in Waco and had been with them on radio KTSA in San Antonio for a while, with a sponsor, which got the group the princely sum of thirty-five dollars a week. Then they got on station WACO in that city and had not only a time slot with a sponsor but also an agent, which was usually a pathway to some success. That's the group they called the Unholy Three, not the group from the Knights of Columbus Hall. When their agent got them on KFJZ in Fort Worth, they decided they needed a new name and selected the "Tune Tinkers." They played a lot on the air, but there was room in the schedule for other acts. And then, in early 1931, Bob, vocalist Milton Brown, and guitarist Herman Arnspiger came in when Alton was serving as KFJZ's acting program director. Bob said they were the Wills Fiddle Band and that they wanted to audition for a spot on the radio. Alton asked him what kind of music they played. Bob said, "Different." They were so unusual and energetic that Alton thought, at first, they were a comedy act, but they were quite serious, and he put them on the air. They started getting fan mail—in fact, more of it than all the other acts on KFJZ at the time—and got on at the station for six days a week at fifteen dollars a week for the whole band. Pretty modest pay on a relatively small station, but it was at least a starting point for greater popularity and success.

In fact, the band got so popular that they were invited to become the promotional group for the Burrus Mill and Elevator Company, millers of Light Crust Flour, which was already a commercial powerhouse not just in the Fort Worth area but throughout large areas of Texas and Oklahoma. The band became known as the Light Crust Doughboys and soon began making personal appearances all over the place and performing on the radio in a hugely popular noontime broadcast on WBAP, one of the broadcasting giants in the Southwest. Before long, the Doughboys were playing over a network of stations in Texas and Oklahoma. As successful as they were, however, trouble was brewing. Almost from the beginning, the band chafed under the leadership of Burrus Mills's general manager, W. Lee O'Daniel, who saw them as a tool for advancing his own ambitions, as well as the success of his flour company. O'Daniel saw himself as something of a poet and songwriter and wanted to appear with the band and read his corny poems and give little talks. He showed his low regard for the band members by making them work in the mill, along with their rigorous rehearsal and performance schedule.

Before long, Bob and a couple of the other guys decided to leave the Doughboys. O'Daniel was powerful enough to make their lives difficult if they stayed in Fort Worth, so they headed to Waco, where WACO carried the Doughboys. Radio listeners in Waco had always shown a strong interest in the music of the Doughboys, and Bob believed his new band would win them over quickly if he could get on WACO. Sure enough, the band, which Bob named the "Playboys," got a broadcasting slot on WACO and things were off to a good start. Bob met a local businessman, O. W. Mayo, who agreed to become his manager. After not much time, though, O'Daniel persuaded the manager of WACO to drop the Playboys or lose the popular Light Crust Doughboys. Bob got the message and decided to leave Waco. A band just couldn't make it without radio support. In one of the luckiest breaks Bob ever got, O. W. Mayo decided to quit his job and go with him. Mr. Mayo saw Bob's potential, and he and the Playboys headed for Oklahoma City, which was also a strong market for the Doughboys. When the same thing as happened with WACO happened with the radio station in Oklahoma City, which buckled under O'Daniel's threats of cancellation, Bob and Mr. Mayo decided to try Tulsa. Fortunately, the management at Tulsa's powerful KVOO decided to go with Bob's band, which he now called the "Texas Playboys," and told the blowhard O'Daniel to get lost. O'Daniel later parlayed the popularity of the Light Crust Doughboys into getting elected governor of Texas and United States senator, but by then Bob was long shed of him. Mr. Mayo established a solid business plan, and by the summer of 1935, Bob Wills and His Texas Playboys were a big deal.

In the meantime, Alton hadn't had as much good fortune in the music business. KFJZ had to lay off several of their full-time staff members, including Alton, and he went back to Waco in the summer of 1932 with his Unholy Three/Tune Tinker buddy Larry White. They played for meals at a place called the Palace of Sweets and then organized what he called an "outlaw" band, that is, non-union. He said he couldn't afford the dues necessary to join the American Federation of Musicians, so, using his Baylor nickname, they called the band "Strick Stricklin and the Outlaws." That didn't last very long, and he ended up going back to the family farm, helping out there, and getting odd jobs. Then suddenly, there was the possibility of full-time work. Late that summer, a friend told Alton about a teaching position near Grandview. He interviewed and got the job at the same time his brother, Benton, got a full-time job at the bank in Grandview. He told me, "We had a big family celebration. We had both gotten good jobs." He started teaching for ninety dollars a month at a one-room school in the Island Grove community near his home in Johnson County. His description of the experience was comical. You could get teaching credentials in those days with just a couple of years of college work. Rural schools relied on finding teachers with that amount of preparation, in much the same way that rural churches often got lightly trained preachers. One of Alton's favorite stories from his brief teaching career at Island Grove was about a time he was drilling the students on the multiplication tables. He was going around the classroom calling on various kids who were old enough to be responsible for multiplication, working on the twos. And he had fallen into the habit of saying, "What's two times two" or "two times three" and so on, except that as he went on awhile, he began cutting some of his words short and saying "tootems" instead of "two times." After he got up to "tootems" twelve, one of the boys said, "Mr. Stricklin, I don't know what 'tootems twelve' is. I don't even know what 'tootems' is!" That was one of the factors that convinced Alton that teaching might not be for him. He played during the summer of 1933 on an unlicensed radio station in Cleburne, LPCT, and got free lodging with a family in town for giving their daughter piano lessons. As he later told the *Cleburne Times-Review*, "The only money I made that summer was playing dances in Glen Rose for $5 a night." That wasn't a lot, but it convinced him that there might be more money to be made in music than in teaching school. Another factor in his decision to abandon a possible teaching career was his marriage, in 1934, to Arbutus Watson, whom he had met in Glen Rose while doing odd jobs. He needed a larger and more dependable income than he could get in a one-room country schoolhouse. The problem was figuring out how to get it.

Then he got his big break. He was playing in Fort Worth with the Hi-Fliers, who were doing three spots a day on KFJZ, along with some dances. During his two summers off from the teaching job at

Island Grove, he had played some with the Hi-Flyers in Fort Worth and worked part-time at KFJZ, making a total of about twenty dollars a week and glad to get it. He was expecting he would have to go back to his teaching job in the fall of 1935, but Bob Wills came back into his life. The Hi-Flyers were playing at a place called the Cinderella Roof on South Jennings Avenue that summer, and Bob came in. They hadn't seen each other in years, but Alton recognized him and, of course, was well aware of the success Bob and his band were having on the radio in Tulsa. During a break, Alton and Bob sat down together, and Bob told him he needed a piano player. Bob had had a piano player, Don Ivey, in the band in Waco and liked what the instrument added to his sound. But Ivey didn't make the transition from Texas to Oklahoma. The Playboys' gifted lead vocalist, Tommy Duncan, knew a little piano and filled in from time to time. Tommy went on to become known as the greatest vocalist in all of western swing, but he didn't sing every song and when he wasn't singing, he would play a little but mostly just bang around on the piano. Bob and the guys in the band, including Tommy, knew they needed someone with more knowledge and skill with chords and rhythm. Bob also mentioned that they were going to be making some records in September and offered Alton thirty dollars a week to join the band, with a five dollar raise every ninety days till he got to fifty dollars a week. Alton was stunned at the offer of so much money, but said he needed to talk it over with his wife. Arbutus was thrilled with the idea, especially the thought of greater financial stability.

Alton wrote Bob, accepted the offer, and got a letter back thanking him for being willing to join his "organization." The letter, which was written on KVOO stationary, said, "I would like to use you in my band, but I don't know whether I could place you in it just now or not." There was a mention of a band Bob's father, John Wills, was playing with, Young John and His Young Five, and that Alton would start off in that band. This was troubling. Bob had talked earlier with Alton about coming to work for him, but the idea of playing in what really would be a fiddle band instead of the fuller, jazzier Texas Playboys didn't seem as encouraging as he had hoped. He had grown up in a house filled with fiddling, but he really considered himself a jazz musician and thought that's where his future lay. Plus, though his wife was excited about the adventure, moving to Tulsa was a big deal and a little scary. Alton and Arbutus had a total of twenty dollars between them and a car they weren't sure would get them all the way to northeastern Oklahoma. They had never lived farther than seventy-five miles from their birthplaces or been outside of Texas. Alton had gotten a telegram earlier that same summer from Louis Welk. This was long before Welk's brother Lawrence became famous. Louis, who had a band in Temple, Texas, addressed the telegram to "Alton Stricklin, Musician, Grandview, Texas." It said, "Need piano man at once. You were recommended to me." The Bob Wills offer was a big gamble, but not as big as taking a job with someone he'd never heard of who had never heard him play. They decided to give Tulsa a try.

CHAPTER 5

A Texas Playboy

When Alton and Arbutus got to Tulsa, he found that his first appearance would be, in fact, with Bob's band, not Bob's father's, so that worry seemed to fade for the moment. Then came the matter of figuring out if he would be accepted by the members of the band and by their rapidly growing number of fans. Fitting in with the band turned out to be a big question. Alton later found out that Bob had put the prospect of playing in his dad's band in his letter to Alton because some of the Playboys had expressed reservations when Bob told them Alton was a "college man" and a schoolteacher. They thought he might be stuck up and wanted to see how he fit in. Bob agreed to keep an eye on the new guy to see how well he could get along with others before accepting him fully. There was also the potential problem of angering Tommy Duncan's fans. His banging around on pianos to cover up the fact that he didn't know much about playing the instrument amused some of their fans, and there was concern that they might miss his clowning.

More importantly, Bob was willing to work very hard, and he hired and kept only band members who shared his dedication. The crushing unemployment during the Great Depression kept most people with jobs highly focused on keeping them. But the members of the Texas Playboys knew they had a good deal: good pay, a boss who wanted them to achieve their creative best, and fellow band members they knew they could count on. They scarcely ever had to cover for someone who wasn't playing well or who wasn't paying attention when Bob called on them to play a solo. Still, it was a grueling lifestyle featuring constant travel on an uncomfortable bus, bumping along on lousy roads to get to dances and other personal appearances, frequent rehearsals to learn and polish songs, and not a lot of time at home. They had to have people they could get along with.

Alton wasn't aware of the concerns about him when he made up his mind to go to Tulsa, but he knew it mattered that he had never been in a band with more than four or five other members before this, certainly nothing with the multiple facets of the Texas Playboys, with their front lineup of twin fiddles—Bob's and, at that time, Jesse Ashlock's—Leon McAuliffe's steel guitar, and Tommy's vocals, along with three horns—Everett Stover on trumpet, Art Haines on trombone, and Robert "Zeb" McNally on saxophone—and a substantial rhythm section, with Herman Arnspiger and C. G. "Sleepy" Johnson on guitars, Bob's brother Johnnie Lee on banjo and his cousin T. C. "Son" Lansford on bass, and W. E. "Smoky" Dacus on drums. That was a lot to try to find your way into. Some of the guys had only been with Bob for a few months, but Alton didn't know that and felt very much like the new kid on the block. Plus, he was only twenty-seven years old. It wasn't like everybody else was aged. Bob was all of thirty. But Alton was wondering if he could pull this off. Just a few minutes into his first show, however, he realized he wasn't going to have to worry about any of that. Bob's personality, charisma, and stage presence picked him up, as it did all the band members, and propelled him into the extraordinary experience of being part of one of the most creative bands in American musical history.

What he had to do was play what Bob wanted, and what Bob wanted was for him to be a strong member of the rhythm section but also to play exciting piano solos when Bob pointed his fiddle bow at him and said to go after it. He quickly realized he was up to that task. Bob saw to the rest, including introducing him to the audience. For that first show, on September 6, 1935, Alton drove straight to the address he'd been given and found Bob and the band playing their live noon radio broadcast from a makeshift stage in the parking lot of a supermarket, the Barrell Food Palace. Alton worked his way through the crowd till Bob spotted him and called out, "Well, look who I see! It's old Al Stricklin. He's a great piano player, and he's coming to work with us. Let him through, folks!" When he got to the piano, he found out it was in terrible shape. He couldn't see how he would be able to get anything worth hearing out of it. But the rest of the band was so strong, and the people were so loud and enthusiastic that they couldn't tell how badly the piano sounded. Nevertheless, he thought, "This may be the end of my short career with Bob Wills," and began thinking about the fact that he and his wife were down to less than fifteen dollars, he'd given up his teaching job, and it would be hard to survive in a town where they didn't know anybody.

Still, he noticed two things. First, Bob had sold him to the crowd, and if Bob could do that with a piano player with a truly terrible piano, he could probably do wonders if the guy had a decent instrument to work with. Second, he noticed that Bob called him "Al." Nobody had ever done that. From then on Alton was Al Stricklin. In time, Bob began to call him "Brother Al" because he knew Al's family were church-going folks, and Bob had a deep respect for that. But on the day of that first show, it was remarkable enough that he got a new name out of a new job. That afternoon the band was set to rehearse. When Al got there, he got an apology from Bob about the lousy piano and Bob's assurance that everybody knew he was going to make a great contribution to their sound. The guys were impressed that Al hadn't thrown a temper tantrum when he tried to play the sorry piano at the Food Palace, and they quickly realized he was a good guy with a sense of humor and a desire to fit in and make some great music. So there he was, in Tulsa, with Bob Wills. He was a Texas Playboy.

Al didn't have much awareness at this early date that he had joined not just a band but a growing business enterprise. Almost immediately upon arriving in Tulsa early in 1934, Bob and O. W. Mayo were able to make a deal with Tulsa's twenty-five-thousand-watt, clear-channel radio station KVOO to get the band on the air, a necessity if they wanted to promote their live appearances. Mr. Mayo was an astute businessman, and he had a good sense of music. In fact, later on, he and Al cowrote one of the songs the band recorded, "Red Hot Gal of Mine." When Bob and Mr. Mayo talked KVOO general manager William Way into giving Bob and the band a spot on the air in February 1934, everybody knew who the Light Crust Doughboys were, but the Texas Playboys were still relatively unknown, so it was a bit of a gamble for Way and KVOO. The gamble paid off quickly, and soon Bob and the boys had a show during the noon hour, which in the 1930s was prime time on radio. By the mid-1930s, more than half the homes in the United States had a radio, and vast numbers of people with those radios ate lunch at home either because they were out of work or they came home from their jobs to have an inexpensive noon meal. Listening to the radio became a national obsession, and a great deal of what people got to hear on the radio in those days was live music, performed in radio studios or on location and picked up for broadcast. Soon, Bob Wills and His Texas Playboys were also broadcasting on KVOO on Thursday and Saturday nights from Cain's Dancing Academy, which took its name from a previous owner who had offered ballroom-dance lessons. It's still an active venue, now known as Cain's Ballroom. As their popularity grew, Bob and the band worked a regular circuit of venues out of town, especially in Oklahoma City, Wichita, Kansas, and Fort Smith, Arkansas, along with many smaller places. The live broadcasts on KVOO made it essential for the band to get back to Cain's from wherever they had played, no matter how grueling the travel, and they sometimes drove through the night and into the morning to make that noontime radio show. This was part of the inspiration for the 1941 song "Take Me Back to Tulsa."

As their popularity grew, Bob and the Playboys generated more and more advertising revenue, which created more opportunities. On the foundation of regular personal appearances and being able to promote them over KVOO, Bob and Mr. Mayo created other enterprises around Bob and his band. It was only logical that one of their most important business ventures would involve bread. Flour and bread companies had been sponsors of live music practically since the beginning of radio. This was especially true in the American "heartland," where audiences tended to be made up of people with modest incomes. If you were one of those people during the Great Depression, bread was a big part of your diet. Even the poorest people bought bread, and most of them listened to the radio. Burrus Mills and the Light Crust

Doughboys had worked to appeal to this market, and Bob and Mr. Mayo were determined to follow that model. They negotiated a licensing agreement with Red Star Milling Company of Wichita to bring out Play Boy Flour. Bob and the band promoted the flour on their broadcasts and used a variety of marketing gimmicks such as "favorite" recipes assigned to each band member, usually a baked item the Texas Playboy whose name was on it had never heard of, let alone eaten. The Play Boy Flour deal was sealed in September 1935, the same month Bob and the band made their first phonograph recordings for American Record Corporation/ Columbia Records in Dallas.

Just a little over two weeks after joining the band, Al was off with the group to Dallas to make those first recordings. He already knew some of the songs they were going to record, but several were new to him. Crucial to Al's progress in learning quickly how to be in Bob's band was the drummer, Smoky Dacus, who befriended him and gave him advice about how Bob wanted a song's beat to work. When they got to Dallas, they set up in a warehouse at 508 Park Avenue. It wasn't a recording studio, just a big building with some empty space in it. The recordings were made with one microphone, which meant everybody had to circle around it, with some instruments closer and others, such as the drums, farther away. It seems impossibly primitive now, thinking about how many elements of music-making engineers and producers can control with current technology. But the legendary field recording specialist and English native Art Satherley and his colleagues were in charge of Bob's Dallas sessions and had made musical recordings in people's houses and church halls and, in fact, other warehouses. They were artists themselves, just as surely as were the people whose music they were recording. There were nice studios in New York and Chicago, but Satherley's talent scouts and engineers went around the country recording people who probably weren't ever going to make it to a big-city studio. Everyone who loves American music is in their debt. And in September 1935, no one knew if the session with Bob Wills and His Texas Playboys was going to be their first and last or if they were going to end up recording in Chicago or New York someday. As it turned out, their next sessions were in Chicago, in 1936, but that might not have seemed very likely when the first session got started on September 23, a sweltering Monday morning in Dallas.

Bob was very hot natured, as was Al, which can be seen in photos from those days. They are often pictured soaked with sweat. The Dallas recording crew got some blocks of ice and a couple of fans to try to cool things down a bit. Of course, the band played many venues, not one with air conditioning, so they were used to being hot. But the floor of the building where they were recording, which was not quite the size of a basketball court, didn't have any cross breeze to speak of, and the heat was just miserable. There was also the fact that a lot was riding on these recordings, and some of the guys were a little nervous. It's true that there wasn't a lot of money at stake. Record companies have always had the upper hand in their dealings with artists. Nobody, not even Bob, stood to profit gigantically from record sales, at least until their later megahit "San Antonio Rose." But records mattered because they kept people thinking about the band and wanting to hear them play on the radio, which generated advertising revenue, and in person, which created ticket sales. The spin-off businesses Bob and O. W. Mayo were developing went on to include a rodeo they launched in Tulsa in 1939, the Bob Wills Stampede, and even movie appearances, beginning in 1940 when he and some of the

Texas Playboys made their first movie, *Take Me Back to Oklahoma*, with cowboy superstar Tex Ritter. But in 1935, they needed to have records, if only to prove that they were something to reckon with, and that's why their two-day Columbia session in Dallas in September 1935 mattered.

Bob had made a couple of recordings in Dallas in 1929 with Herman Arnspiger and a couple more in 1932 with Milton and Durwood Brown and Sleepy Johnson, so he had a little experience with making records. Most of the guys in the band didn't. They always said they started with a fast instrumental number called "Osage Stomp" because it was the most difficult song they played. They figured once they got it under their belts the rest of their songs would be a snap. "Osage Stomp" starts with a twin-fiddle line, followed by a loud thump-thump played by the whole rest of the band, rhythm section and all. Then Bob plays a verse of the song by himself. His famous talking during songs shows up at this session, calling out to soloists, commenting on lyrics being sung by one of the other guys, reciting lines from medicine show routines he had learned years before. When you're listening to the band, if a fiddler is playing and Bob isn't saying anything, that means either Bob's the one playing or he's mad at Jesse Ashlock, who was a gifted musician but who was also full of mischief. In this case, it's Bob playing, but very soon Jesse has a solo and, at least on this occasion, wasn't in the doghouse and gets a shout-out from Bob. There's a solo by Leon McAuliffe on his steel guitar, a wild section with the horns, a pounding slap-bass solo by Son Lansford, another chorus, and then the whole business stops as suddenly as it started. The engineers had to stop a couple of times to adjust for the thump-thump at the start of the song, but the Playboys got through the song and made the cut on the second take. In that two-day session, they went on to record such familiar tunes as "I Can't Give You Anything But Love," "St. Louis Blues," "Mexicali Rose," "I Ain't Got Nobody," "Old Fashioned Love," and "Sittin' on Top of the World," along with several others, including two that became Wills standards, "Spanish Two Step" and "Maiden's Prayer." These recordings with Art Satherley catapulted Bob and the band into a new league of professional prominence. A band had to have records to round out the marketing triangle—recordings, radio programs, and live appearances—that helped make a band popular and kept people interested. In that sense, the Dallas sessions in 1935 were a big success.

Even more than with their recordings, though, the band's popularity rose dramatically because of the partnership between Tulsa's radio station KVOO and Bob's home base at Cain's. Everybody listened to KVOO, and, because of that, everybody wanted to go to Cain's. It was where the "Bob Wills Dance" became famous, and the times in which it became famous had a lot to do with its fame. In the Great Depression, especially in Oklahoma and other states where the Playboys' KVOO broadcasts were heard, there weren't a lot of opportunities to have fun. Happiness was something most people couldn't afford. But if you could pull together the small admission price to go to a Bob Wills dance, you would get at least a four-hour respite from the misery and discouragement of the Depression. In the 1930s, dancing was an extremely popular form of entertainment, and once phonograph recordings and radio made singers and bands known in widespread areas, people wanted to see these bands in person and dance to their music. By the time broadcast networks were up and running in the early 1930s, and growing numbers of households had radios, throngs of people were listening to the great "hotel bands" broadcasting live from the ballrooms of famous hotels in big cities, especially New York, Chicago, New Orleans, Dallas, and Los Angeles. Most people in the middle part of the country knew they would never be able to go to one of those live big-city hotel broadcasts, but many of them could get to a dance closer to home. In Oklahoma and in towns in adjoining states in the 1930s and '40s, very often that dance was a Bob Wills dance.

For Bob Wills and His Texas Playboys, a dance hall was their natural habitat. And they gave their fans a full evening's fun every time they played, going through a remarkable variety of tunes over the course of the four hours most of his dances lasted. But those dances provided something that might not have been on offer in countless other dances. Bob and the Playboys gave the dancers their total attention. It's often been said that Bob and the band weren't after applause. For years, they barely paused between numbers, and the entire band never took a break as a group. The band members would get down one at a time to go to the bathroom and so on, but the music just kept driving on. They scarcely ever had a set list, and they seldom used "head" arrangements, memorized plans to keep track of the sequence of vocals and solos and so on as songs went along. Mainly Bob arranged as songs unfolded. When they finished one song, he might call out the title of the next song and count off four beats, or just start playing, and off again they'd go. What he wanted was dancing. That was how he knew he and the band were engaging the crowd. And whatever they played, from fiddle tunes to novelty numbers to the latest pop hits to blues songs, no matter how slow or fast, every song had to have a beat people could dance to—a happy song, a sad song, it didn't matter. It had to make people want to dance. They even did a two-step version of the "William Tell

Overture"! Bob watched the crowd and picked songs he thought would get people out on the floor. He arranged as the night went on, requiring band members to know the key and the tempo of every song and be ready to go at the first notes, and calling on band members to play solos at a split-second's notice. No gaps, no "dead" time, only enjoyment being provided to people who were hard-bitten by the Depression and who needed a lift, a lift Bob was determined to give them. Despite the popularity of his radio broadcasts, the success of his records, and his many appearances in films and, later, on television, the dance hall was where he made his name. And one place stood out from all the others: Tulsa's Cain's Academy. Anybody who knows about Bob Wills and His Texas Playboys probably knows about them because of what they did at Cain's. That's where they became famous.

In John Wooley and Brett Bingham's fine book on Cain's, *Twentieth-Century Honky-Tonk*, they call Cain's the "Carnegie Hall of Western Swing" and tell how it developed from a 1924 auto garage to a 1930 "academy" for ballroom-dancing lessons to the headquarters for Bob and the band and the remote site for their daily noontime broadcasts on KVOO and Saturday night dances, a portion of which would also be broadcast each week. It had a maple floor installed by Madison "Daddy" Cain for better dancing than the original oak floor. Wooley and Bingham debunk the legend that Cain had springs installed under the floor to give dancers an extra "bounce" as they did their steps. Restoration work in 2007 revealed no springs. The fact that so many people believed the legend for decades probably reflects the excitement and enjoyment people felt at Cain's, beginning with that "lift" Bob and the Playboys wanted to give people. It must be said that the crowds at Cain's were often so huge that there wasn't actually enough room to dance, but the fact remains that Cain's Academy, as the guys always called it, was famous because of what everybody called the Bob Wills Dance.

Sadly, there are only a few low-quality live recordings of the music people would have heard at Cain's when Al was with the band, from 1935 to 1942. I've always said that if anybody ever invents a time machine and calls me to ask where I'd like to go, I'll say, "Cain's Academy, 423 North Main Street, Tulsa, Oklahoma, about eight o'clock on a Saturday night. Let's say October 1936." At that point, they were still so new at making this music that I would love to get to hear it. I'll never forget how it felt when I was twenty-seven and listening to recordings of the band and realizing my father was the age I was then when he was helping create this remarkable music. I couldn't imagine doing what he had done, what all those guys had done, with Bob. They were making it up as they went along, devising this exciting new music, drawing influences from all over the place but creating a sound all their own. Others at the time were also doing great things, including others playing what later became known as western swing. But Bob's band was knocking down walls and opening doors that had kept different kinds of music separated and showing that combining all these elements could be enjoyable and popular.

You can get a sense of that quality and creativity from the great recordings they made. In 1935 and '36, the music sounds kind of raw, especially compared to the smoother sound after gigantically important guitarist Eldon Shamblin joined the band in 1937. The fiddles in the earlier band soar, the steel guitar slices the air, the horns sound like a Salvation Army band on amphetamines. And the rhythm section pounds out that essential Bob Wills thing, the beat. On these recordings, you have to listen very carefully to be able to hear Al because the point of a rhythm section for those guys was to play together. Listen especially to the rhythm section in the Playboys' 1937, pre-Eldon recording of "Blue Yodel Number 1," the famous Jimmie Rodgers tune that begins, "T for Texas, T for Tennessee." There's an opening fiddle solo by Bob and then Tommy Duncan's first vocal verse. Then, during Leon McAuliffe's hot steel guitar solo, the drums, piano, rhythm guitars, and bass sound as if they're all one instrument. Only some little piano licks Al puts in between beats with his right hand get out of that groove set by the rhythm section. The point was not to stand out from the others. When any of them got called on to play a solo, that's when they poured it on.

When Al plays a solo, you hear not only the "hot" improvisation he's doing with his right hand but also the "stride" and "walking" rhythm work he's doing with his left, because he's supposed to play a little louder than usual. Hear his solos, for instance, on "Steel Guitar Rag," "Old-Fashioned Love," "Corrine Corrina," and "Twin Guitar Special." The stride method, explained in its simplest terms, is hitting a bass note, then a chord, then a different bass note, and then, most often, the same chord. For instance, if a song is in the key of C, the piano player's left hand would hit the C an octave or so below Middle C on the keyboard, then a C chord up an octave or two, then the single note G back in the first octave, then the C chord again, and so on, continuing that pattern as the song's chords changed. That alternating bass style created a strong floor for the piano player's left hand but also for the rest of the musicians as they were working their way through the song.

Music writers often commented on Al's strong left hand. As a stride piano player, he built everything on that foundation, inspired by the great jazz piano artists, especially Earl Hines. He loved Hines so much that his great friend in the Playboys, drummer Smoky Dacus, called him "Father," riffing a bit on Hines's nickname "Fatha." Al loved Hines because they both loved the left hand, and he marveled at Hines's huge reach of bass notes. He told me, "Hines would hit a C with his little finger and hit the G above the next C with his thumb, which was an octave and a half—I mean all at the same time. And to get an idea of how far that is to reach, try it sometime!" Hines also brought to every song the kind of timing that makes the piano such a great instrument to play in a dance band. But that's not the only source of Al's piano style.

His love of Earl Hines and other fine stride piano players was huge, but the music writers never knew that Al got a lot of his left-hand style, the sense of movement—some of his "walking" bass style—from his sister, Violet. Because of her bout with scarlet fever as a young girl and accompanying brain damage, she had some conversational and personal habits that tried people's patience. She never had a real job for more than a few days at a time, and she just never got to do much with her life. But Violet had a great sense of humor—she once gave me an old pocketknife and told me it was "as sharp as a hammer"—and she had quite a bit of musical talent. Al always said if she could have had some training and hadn't had her mental limitations, she would have been a better musician than he was. With her left hand, she played with a simple, three-finger chord style. My sister Judy always talks about Aunt Violet's one-two-three bass style. It wasn't much to listen to, but I think it planted some of the seeds of the trademark Stricklin left hand. Aunt Violet would play something like an arpeggio, playing the notes in a chord one at a time instead of all at once, what's sometimes called a "rolled" chord—but she kept the chords going and, I think, probably gave Al a sense that his left hand could do something more than just go up and down. And when Al played the piano, he used pretty much all of the keyboard. His left hand would cover three octaves, often employing the stride style of alternating bass chords with single notes but also using various "walking" patterns during which he'd move his left hand, usually step-by-step up the scale, during each chord change. His left hand would be heading toward the center of the keyboard while his right hand started high and also worked toward the middle. A lot of this came from Aunt Violet's example.

He did something with his right hand that he knew was unusual but couldn't really explain, only to say that it probably resulted from his relative lack of formal musical instruction. He told me in an interview,

> I was the most informal piano player you ever heard. I didn't do anything according to how it ought to be done! In the first place, every other piano player I ever heard plays the melody note high. I play the melody note low, with my thumb, which is as unorthodox as you could be. It's like scratching your nose with your big toe! That's why nearly everybody that's ever heard me play, they'll say, "That's old Al Stricklin playing that piano." That's why nobody sounds like me. It's not good, but it's different!

•••

There were other ways that his style showed the influences of his family from the days when he was learning to play and perfecting his style and his unfailing sense of rhythm, which came in handy when he joined the Texas Playboys. As he told me,

> Bob played a whole lot like my father, and I could tell by the way he thumped his fingers on those strings before he started what key he was gonna play in and whether it was gonna be fast or slow. Without my long experience of playing with my father like that, I probably would have been lost when I went to work for Bob.

But Al's adaptation to the band also reflected the ways he and Smoky Dacus developed their musical partnership in the rhythm section of the Texas Playboys. Smoky, who was one of the most entertaining people I was ever around, had a strong dislike of fussy playing. He was the captain of the Playboy rhythm section and modeled what everybody ought to do by getting in the groove and staying put. He told me in an interview that he enjoyed the challenge of creating a beat for the rhythm section of what Bob started out with, which was essentially a string band. He said, "At that time, a set of drums was unheard of" in that kind of band. Smoky thought Bob was out of his mind when he asked him to join the band. Smoky said he asked Bob,

> "What would a drummer play?" Of course, at that time in '35, you could eat all you wanted in the best places in Tulsa for fifteen cents. Bob wanted to pay me fifty-five dollars a week. "There ain't nobody that makes that much money!" The boys in the hotel band I played with were skeptical. Most of them made fun of me. "You're gonna play drums in a fiddle band?" And that was my biggest problem: What sounds good? So I tried to develop a sound that fit. For fifty-five dollars a week, you'd work at it! It wasn't long before I found the freedom in this kind of music that wasn't in the other music. The big bands that sat up there with the music in front of them, they played as if they were mummies. Their only concern was the notes

> in front of them. You could dance by in front of them, and they wouldn't even see you. But in Bob's band, music was communication. I know a lot of musicians that you could take a bottle of ink and throw it against the wall and bust it. And they can pick up a trumpet and play it. Wouldn't make any difference what kind of mess it made, they could play it. But you put them at the end of a hundred-foot rope, and they couldn't swing. No feeling!

Keeping in mind the central requirement to keep the beat going so people could dance to the song they were playing, Smoky and Al played *to* each other, not just *with* each other. They worked together for almost seven years, and during that time they recorded more than two hundred songs with Bob and the band, and I estimate that they played more than two thousand radio broadcasts and probably that many more dances and other personal appearances. Even with the excitement of the constant possibility that Bob would point his fiddle bow at you for your solo and expect you to do something special, playing that much could be a grind. Al and Smoky developed little games and special rhythmic tricks that were like messages they sent out during the long nights of four-hour dances, sometimes signals about how one of them thought the song should change. Smoky even had a little riff he would play on the drums at the end of one of Al's solos, sometimes three beats, sometimes four, as if to say, "Good job, Father." A good example is what Smoky does at the end of Al's solo on the 1936 version of "Steel Guitar Rag." Al starts as Bob says, "Look out, Al Stricklin now" and ends as Smoky hits his three trademark beats.

I got to hear the band often after they got back together in the '70s, and I liked to position myself by the back corner of the bandstand where I could see Smoky and Al, the looks on their faces, the strange ways their hands would begin to move up and down on the drums and the piano. It wasn't the way you usually see people play those instruments but more like they were coaxing sound out of them, with fluid, graceful motions that somehow managed to create a rhythm of great power. Smoky nearly always played with a brush in his left hand and a stick in his right, and every now and then he would find something to hit so he could create what he called the "suitcase rhythm," which he said he first discovered one time when he didn't have a stool to sit on and was using one of his drum cases for a seat. It occurred to him at one point to whack the side of that case, which created a beat so strong, he told me in an interview, "The frequency of it was such that you could hear it three blocks before you got close enough to the dance hall to hear the music. It just cut like a knife." Getting the beat "right down in the bottom of that V," he said, "Why, you could go to lunch and come back, and it would still be there." The rest of the night, and for many other appearances, he would hit the side of that case, which he thought must have made him look like a jockey using a crop on a racehorse. When they were playing with Bob, they knew better than to undermine what Bob thought should be going on, but they had fun playing around with beats and timing. Smoky and Al played a lot of music together during their two times in the band and had a lot of practice reading each other's thoughts. They were also the classic professionals, making something very difficult look easy. Their devotion to rhythm that was strong but nonetheless relaxed exemplified one of Bob's rules for music, "Nothing forced or fancy," an approach that relied on playing in the moment, not being stuck on someone else's understanding of the music. The ways the drummer and the bass player and the piano player are playing or the ways the steel guitar and the six-string guitar players are playing a duet, the beauty of how those great arrangements unfold and how the rhythm section works with the soloists—both singers and fiddlers and other instrumentalists—it's all just magnificent. It's art, for people who often don't think they like art. And the fact that it was put together for the most part by people who didn't have a lot of formal training makes it even more interesting. They were able to create something imaginative and pathbreaking that also happens to be a lot of fun. All you have to do is listen to the recordings from the period when Al was with the Playboys, 1935–42, to know that they were having some fun. It was hard work, especially with the traveling—and Bob was a demanding bandleader—but he was demanding in just the way a creative person wants a leader to be demanding. Bob expected everybody in the band to play to their highest ability, and in the process, he made them household names throughout much of the United States and beyond.

This whole creative feeling, the thing Smoky described, was central to Bob's dances. Many people would stand in front of the bandstand, watching instead of dancing, fascinated by the way Bob worked. He was an accomplished fiddler, but he made a name for himself as a band leader, and he was the absolute master of the Texas Playboys. People would reach up to shake his hand and pat him on the back. He was constantly making eye contact with the customers, sizing up the crowd, deciding what number to call next. The guys in the band kept their eyes on Bob constantly, ready at a moment's notice to take a solo or come up and sing a verse or a whole song. People always said his dark eyes exerted an almost hypnotic effect on the crowd. And the musicians, who never knew exactly what would happen next, were certain that they would be there to give the song everything they had when their turn came to play a solo, what they called a "break." Veteran Texas Playboys always advised newcomers to the band, "When it's time for you to take a break, play all you know." Al told me his attitude was, "When he points at me and says, 'Brother Al Stricklin now,' with that smile on his face, I'm just gonna hit whatever gets in my way." To be with that band at that time, when they were so creative and so unpredictable, was a wonderful, liberating experience.

In the world of Bob Wills, you had to be ready to go where he wanted you to go. If they had had written arrangements that governed each song every time they played it, it would have been easier for a new member of the band to follow along. But that wasn't the idea. Though they didn't have many head arrangements, they knew what had worked the last time they did a song and had some generally understood techniques that came in handy, such as the turn-around, vamping, and going around the bend, which Al had taught his Waco piano students. Sometimes somebody would call out those terms so a newcomer to the band could get some help knowing what was coming up next and what to do. But a lot of the time they just felt it and knew.

Al was one of the guys in the band who made friends with black musicians in Tulsa. Bob had a lifelong interest in blues, especially the music of the great Bessie Smith, who strongly influenced his singing style, and the Playboys knew they might pick up some techniques from black bands that would please their boss. They also wanted to keep up with the latest trends in popular music, partly because they were busily creating some of those trends, and partly because, like all musicians, they were always on the lookout for ideas they could learn from other players and singers. Mostly, what they got from other bands came from records they got their hands on. That's how they kept up with new songs, hot players, and interesting arrangements by popular groups and solo artists from other parts of the country, as well as foreign musicians such as the remarkable duo of Django Reinhardt and Stephane Grappelli. They could have heard other musicians on the radio, especially the big bands that broadcast live shows from hotel ballrooms in large cities, but the Playboys were usually working when those shows were on the air. Another source of keeping up was what the musicians called "sweating out" other bands. Some of the guys would go to listen to other groups play after they got off work at Cain's, which sometimes made the musicians they went to hear a little nervous, knowing they were being scrutinized by their peers. Through this habit, they got to hear some of the most exciting music in America, especially being played by black bands.

Like most segregated American cities in those days, Tulsa had rules against "race mixing." And people there were still on edge in the mid-1930s because of the terrible race massacre that had occurred in Tulsa in 1921. But there were loopholes in the rules. African Americans were prohibited from attending events at "white" venues such as Cain's, but white people were free to go to "black" venues. That double standard made it possible for members of the Texas Playboys to hear some of the era's great black bands that came to Tulsa, led by Duke Ellington, Fats Waller, Count Basie, and others. Musicians could always tell when others had come to sweat them out in those days when bands nearly always consisted completely of men. A small group of men sitting by themselves, no dance partners visible, just watching and listening to the visiting band never failed to attract notice, especially a small group of white guys in a black club. Sweating out another band was considered a compliment. After working a long night, you wouldn't go check out another band unless you really thought you could learn something from watching and hearing them play. Often, the musicians would visit during breaks. Al met his hero, Earl Hines, that way. Also, the great Fats Waller. After a break at his show, Waller asked Al to sit with him on his bench as he played. He told him he'd heard records of the Texas Playboys and said, "You guys have got it going on!"

As they were developing all of this, KVOO strengthened its status as a broadcasting powerhouse. Its signal was heard all over the central part of North America and could be picked up at night as far away as California. Because Bob called out to his vocalists and to the guys doing instrumental solos, people who listened to them on the radio and on records got to know their names. There were a few well-known featured musicians in other big bands, mainly vocalists, but Bob called out the names of so many of his band members that anybody who listened regularly could name at least a handful of the guys and often more than that. Al got a letter early in 1938 from a family who said, "We named our baby boy after you because he was born on your birthday!" That meant, of course, that they not only knew Al's name but also knew the date of his birth, because of Bob. Steel guitarist Leon McAuliffe became so famous that U.S. service personnel in the Pacific theater of World War II said he made it into the list of taunts Japanese troops would use to try to demoralize their American foes, yelling out at night, "Go to hell, Babe Ruth! Go to hell, Betty Grable! Go to hell, Leon!" Sometimes, Bob would not call out a guy's name, particularly if the musician had just joined the band or if Bob was mad at him. Fiddler Jesse Ashlock went on and off the band repeatedly. Bob would get mad at him and fire him, then hire him back. Sometimes he wasn't mad enough to fire him, just mad enough not to call Jesse's name. But I was always pleased that every time Al played a solo on any of the recordings from the 1930s and '40s, if Bob was present for the session he always said my father's name: "Look out Al Stricklin now" or "Here's Brother Al Stricklin, the old piano pounder" and the like.

The fact that Al's name was known was the source of one of his favorite stories. He was home in Texas for a few days off and riding across Johnson County with his brother, Benton. They came upon a young man hitchhiking and pulled over to give him a ride. In the Depression, so many people were down on their luck that many drivers picked people up without giving it a second thought. The young man was very friendly and very grateful for the ride. Benton was driving and turned around to welcome the hitchhiker, who said, "Thanks for picking me up. What do you fellows do?" Benton said, "Well, I work for the newspaper in Cleburne, and my brother here is a musician." Before Benton had a chance to say anything else about his musician brother in the front seat with him, the young man blurted out, "Well, isn't that a coincidence?! I'm a musician, too. In fact, you might have heard of me. I'm old Brother Al Stricklin with the Texas Playboys!" Benton, who like Al had a dry and quick wit, said, "You know, I have heard of Al Stricklin. Tell us all about it!" And the poor kid launched into a long story about how great it was to travel around with the band and what a great boss Bob Wills was and how much fun it was to be on the radio and have people all over the place know who you are. The young man figured that they were far enough away from the band's headquarters in Tulsa that he could get away with saying he was one of the famous Texas Playboys, and Al and his brother, who both loved practical jokes, let the poor guy dig himself in deeper and deeper with tales of playing with the legendary

Bob Wills. Finally, they came to the crossroads where the young man needed to get out, and without ever addressing the obvious question—if you're this famous musician, how come you have to bum rides to get around the county?—the hitchhiker said, "I never did catch you fellows' names." Al said, "Hey, you're right. Let me show you my union card." And he pulled it out of his billfold and showed the card to the Al wannabe: "Alton M. Stricklin, American Federation of Musicians, Tulsa Local 94." The poor kid's eyes got as big as platters, Al always said, and he jumped out of the car and took off running.

As unlikely as it might seem to run across someone pretending to *be* him, Al always told that story to make the point that this was the power of Bob Wills, the reach of their radio broadcasts, and the fact that people felt that Bob and the members of the band were their friends. The kid had heard Bob call out Al's name on the radio, probably lots of times, but had never seen Al in person, so he could imagine Al any way he wanted, even turning himself into a version of Al. It was also a great example of being in the wrong place at the wrong time and of the way he and his brother could let a joke unfold without having to say a word.

CHAPTER 6

Johnnie and Betty

Like everybody in the band, Al had a home life that often took a back seat to work, the demanding schedule of learning and rehearsing new songs, daily radio broadcasts, constant travel to dances and shows, and countless promotional appearances at groundbreaking events for businesses and schools, all kinds of things. He once said that the guys figured it up one time and estimated that they spent two-thirds of their time with each other. In an interview in the *Music City News*, Leon McAuliffe told about the band's grueling work schedule:

> We played dances six nights a week. Two were in town, and the other four were within a 200-mile radius. We'd leave at 4:00 p.m. on a Tuesday, for example, and get back to Tulsa at 4:00 a.m. Wednesday. We'd sleep for a while and then do our noon radio show every day. After each show was over, we'd rehearse.

It was hard work but a happy life for Al. Just about anybody with a job during the Great Depression had the sense of having a good life. That was especially true of Al when his wife gave birth to Nancy in 1937. As Nancy told me in an interview, Bob asked Al "what he wanted to play for his new baby daughter. It was during their daily radio show, and he said he thought about all the bills they had facing them and told Bob he wanted to play 'I Can't Give You Anything But Love,'" which the Playboys had recorded on the first day of their first recording session, in 1935. In Texas, Nancy's mother had gone by Arbutus, her given name. But in Oklahoma, she called herself Johnnie, which seemed to mean she had become a different person, possibly because Johnnie's mother was difficult to be around, and Johnnie was relieved to be away from some of the drama at home. She and Al played tennis and golf together and rode bicycles and had a great time. Then she got sick with cancer and died early in 1941. It was a shocking thing. She was always vibrant, energetic, and athletic, with a positive, fun attitude. The first time Al ever saw her, Nancy recalled, he was doing one of the odd jobs he got from time to time, using a skill he had picked up from his father, back on the farm:

> He was grafting pecan trees at Glen Lake Park—near Glen Rose, Texas—and playing piano at Oak Dale Park at night. He was up in a tree, and when he looked down, he saw a skinny young girl, hands on hips. She wanted to know what he was doing. My mother played church league basketball. Her diary talks about meeting his family, and when she went to Tarleton State College to school, Daddy wrote to her giving words of advice about being a good girl and staying out of trouble. She finished the first semester and started the second. They were married in the front parlor of the log portion of the old Benton home near Grandview.

Nancy's birth was a major event in the Stricklin family. The Bentons of Al's parents' generation were not big on having children. Al's mother, Annie, was one of seven children, but of the six who lived to adulthood, she was the only one to have any children. The twins, John and Will, never married, nor did their sister Lochie. Other sisters Cora and Bertie married but never had kids. Of Annie's three children, only one—Al—had kids. Violet never married, Benton got married well into his thirties to a distant cousin and never had children. When Benton told Al he was planning to marry, he said he hoped Al wouldn't disapprove because it might dishonor the memory of their late mother. Al never understood that, since he himself was already married. But he thought it reflected the fact that Benton was a tender soul.

Then, after a shockingly short time fighting a form of skin cancer, Johnnie was gone.

Nancy said,

> I do not remember her at all, but I do remember having to be quiet in the house because she was ill. On the morning after she died, I awoke to a house in confusion. Daddy was moving out. He would not spend another night in the house. I asked my grandmother where my mother was, and she told me, "The angels came in the night and took her away." I thought that was kind of neat, but she didn't tell me they were not bringing her back. I was three, and my mother was twenty-five.

Nancy and Al benefitted from the help of the guys in the band and their wives. Nancy's middle name is Jo, after Texas Playboy Joe Ferguson, who was her godfather. Joe and his wife helped take care of Nancy and the household during Johnnie's decline. Nancy said Smoky Dacus was there when Johnnie died and that she stayed with Tommy Duncan and his wife for several days. Bob gave Al several hundred dollars for Johnnie's funeral and burial in the family plot at Antioch, back in Texas. When Al got back to Tulsa and went to talk to

Bob about arranging repayment of what he thought was a loan, Bob told him it wasn't a loan. It was a gift. Al told often about tearing up because of Bob's generosity, which he knew Bob extended to countless other people over the years. Bob gave money and jobs and other help to no telling how many people who were down on their luck. And he would take a vocal quartet from the band, along with Al to accompany them on the piano, and sing at funerals of fans. Bob promoted charitable causes in Tulsa, both in person and on the radio. Al always said that Bob did most of these things so quietly that very few people knew about them, other than the recipients of his generosity.

•••

While Al was getting established in Tulsa and getting to experience the height of the popularity of the Texas Playboys, Betty Jo Zeigler was finishing up her teen years nearby, in the town of Hominy, in Osage County. Headed toward her birthday, in November, she was just thirteen years old in September 1935, the month Al started with the band at the age of twenty-seven. Betty had something of a turbulent upbringing, especially with regard to her father, William Robert Forrest Lee Zeigler. He may have been an interesting man. He was a pharmacist, a Spanish-American War veteran, and an avid traveler. But his travels featured long disappearances that added to the difficulty Betty's family faced making it through the Great Depression. It was hard enough to get by during the economic catastrophe of the 1930s and harder for a single-parent family, which they essentially were. Betty's account of these events always included her description of how her father would disappear for months at a time, sometimes years, and return long enough to get her mother pregnant. This pattern produced six children in the Hominy, Oklahoma, home. Their father was largely unknown apart from the fact that he once said if he'd had another uncle, he would have had another middle name. Betty's mother, Bethel Miller Zeigler, was a nurse. All the kids got part-time jobs as soon as they were old enough.

There were those who thought Betty's father had another family off somewhere, possibly in Virginia, where he had relatives. In any event, his long absences created a lot of tension. Betty said that one time when she was about five, she was walking by herself in Hominy's downtown. It was a small town, and everybody knew everybody else, so her mother let her wander around on her own. Suddenly, she saw a man at a distance coming toward her. He looked familiar, but she was a little uneasy as he got closer, and then she realized it was her father. She hadn't seen him in many months, what probably amounted at that time to one tenth of her life. As he got close enough to her to speak, he said, "I don't know which one you are, but I know you're a Zeigler."

Betty's sister Ann got along with their father better than the other kids and could stand up to him in some ways, which taxed his patience. On one occasion several years after the encounter on the streets of Hominy, Betty was coming up the steps to their front door just as her father came storming out of it. She told me years later that she was in a particularly good mood about something fun that had happened or was going to. She was even whistling as she hopped up to the front door of the house. She later found out her father had been having an argument with Ann and had lost his temper and was on his way, who knows where, when he stomped out of the house and encountered Betty. He said, "What are you so happy about?" Then he backhanded her and knocked her off the front porch. No one said or did anything about it. He was gone before long anyway. But it didn't seem right to Betty that he was mad at Ann and took it out on her. That kind of thing made Betty think carefully about getting away, which all her siblings ended up doing. The two brothers went into the Army. One of the sisters moved to California. Another married and settled nearby, in Barnsdall, which is also in Osage County but wasn't Hominy. Ann had a failed first marriage and then married a guy who was career military. They had a long marriage and lived in lots of places, including Japan. But nobody stayed in the old hometown. And, as far as I ever knew, Betty never whistled again. I certainly never heard her.

Betty knew there wasn't much chance that any of the kids would get to go to college. It wasn't any picnic before the Great Depression set in, and it was certainly tight after that. So she went to work at the age of twelve, mainly in a drugstore in Hominy, while finishing the public schools there. She had a good head for numbers and began to think that she might try to get a job someday working in a business office. She didn't even know how to think about having a career. Getting a job would be plenty. She picked up little bits of money here and there doing other jobs, one of which led to her first meeting with her future husband, my father.

Betty's brother Roland was in the National Guard before World War II started, and he was in charge of the armory in Hominy. He helped make the arrangements when people wanted to hold events there. In those days, there were National Guard armories all over the place, providing a headquarters for Guard members who lived close by to gather and get training and information. In lots of little towns, the National Guard armory was the biggest meeting place, and Guard commanders were usually generous about letting people use armory buildings. On this occasion, which would have been around 1940, the Texas Playboys were going to play a dance at the armory in Hominy. And Uncle Roland hired Betty to take tickets to earn a little extra money. She got there early and was on the job when the band pulled up and the Playboys got off the bus and started inside the armory to get set up. She recognized Bob, of course. His picture was in newspapers all over northeastern Oklahoma. And she knew the names of most of the members of the band, like everybody did who listened to them on the radio, because of the ways Bob called on them and said things about them. But she didn't recognize most of the guys in the band. They were all—well, almost all—carrying instruments, though, so she didn't say anything to anybody about needing a ticket to get in, until Al came walking up. Bob never took a piano to appearances with the band. It would have been a nightmare to lug a heavy thing like a piano around, but that meant Al was always at the mercy of whatever instrument the local folks setting up for the dance or the concert could manage to get to the venue. One time he even got stuck trying to play an old pump organ at a show, with hilarious and disastrous results. At the armory in Hominy, Uncle Roland had probably been involved in making sure there was a piano on hand, but Betty didn't know about any of that and asked Al for his ticket. He said, "I don't need a ticket. I'm with the band." She said, "How do I know that? Where's your instrument?" He said, "I'm Al Stricklin. I'm the piano player. The piano is already here, or at least it's supposed to be." They went back and forth for a time. Finally, Bob realized what was going on and vouched for Al and got the nice young lady to let him in. Our family has always laughed about the fact that the first time Al and Betty ever saw each other they had an argument.

Like many broadcasting performers, Wills invited listeners to send him postcards requesting dedications of various songs in honor of friends and loved ones. The practice kept people listening, in case their request got on the air. Bob was very serious about collecting these requests and tried to get to as many of them as possible. The people who sent them in were probably some of his most devoted fans. But requests also gave sponsors a sense of how broadly the broadcasts, and thus their brand names, were being heard. Cards came in from dozens of states. The gimmick created at least one poignant moment, on the night of Saturday, December 6, 1941. The request sheet for that night's show had forty-two dedications on three pages and named people in fifteen states. It also listed four U.S. service personnel stationed near Honolulu, Hawaii, three who were aboard ships at Pearl Harbor. The first time I saw that request list for December 6, 1941, I was stunned by the connections to the terrible battle. People listening to the Texas Playboys that night were thinking about loved ones in the service without knowing that, the next day, those loved ones were going to find themselves in a hellish surprise attack. But I was also stunned by request number thirty-three, from some people I'd never heard of in Artesia, New Mexico, for the band to play "Cherokee Maiden" in honor of Betty Jo Zeigler, Tulsa, Oklahoma, Al's future wife. By the end of 1941, she was living in a small apartment and taking business classes in Tulsa. Of course, everything changed the day after the December 6 Playboys broadcast.

When the U.S. entered the war, most of the guys, Bob included, either went into the service or went into defense work. I always thought it was a shame that Glenn Miller, whom I admired a lot, got to be an officer and lead an Army Air Corps band, while Bob was consigned to being an enlisted man. This might have had something to do with the fact that Bob was not a college graduate and that western swing wasn't as highly regarded as the mainstream swing music that Miller's "orchestra" was so well regarded for playing. As the war went on, an airplane Miller was flying in disappeared over the English Channel, and Bob went on to have a long career after it was over, but it never seemed quite fair to me as a youngster listening to stories about the bands and the war and all. Nancy said in an interview that, because of her, the armed services wouldn't take Al. He was a widower with a small child. Essentially, he had a draft exemption to do defense work. In 1942, Al and Nancy moved to Fort Worth, and he went to work at the North American Aircraft plant in Grand Prairie. The plant manager was a fan of the Texas Playboys and made Al a foreman, something Al always said he wasn't very well fitted for, though he was grateful to be off the assembly line and doing something that paid a little more.

A lot happened in a hurry. Bob joined the Army and played his last job with the pre-war band on Christmas Day 1942. Al was already gone by then, as were Smoky, Leon, and several others who went into the service. Being in the military didn't suit someone as strong-willed as Bob, and he and the Army agreed to part company. Bob was a little on the high end of the age group for entry-level service, having been born in 1905, and after a while, the Army concluded that he'd be of greater danger to the Axis powers leading a band and selling war bonds than he would be following orders as a foot soldier. Maybe Bob had been a band leader for too long.

Al played some pickup jobs with bands in and around Fort Worth while working at the aircraft plant. And Betty Zeigler, his argument partner from the job back at the National Guard Armory in Hominy, Oklahoma, also moved to Fort Worth. They had finally met for real and had kept up with each other over the previous year or so. When Bob got out of the service, he invited Al to rejoin the band, but Al couldn't leave his defense work while the war was still on. And Betty, who had a job at the Army depot in Fort Worth, wasn't keen on the idea of going back to her old haunts in Oklahoma. She wanted to give the Fort Worth-Dallas area a try. Nancy recalled that Betty's cousin Lois came with her and said that Betty, Lois, and Al's brother Benton's sister-in-law moved in with Al and Nancy in these up-in-the-air war days. Lois took care of Nancy while everybody else went off to work. The three women shared one bedroom, and Al and Nancy slept in the other one. Once, Nancy said,

> While we were living in Fort Worth, Mother was going somewhere in the car and looked behind her to make sure there was no one there. But a neighbor stopped her before she backed out to ask her about something. She forgot to look again and ran over a child that was behind the car playing with my little peddle car. She went running into the house screaming that she had run over the baby. Daddy thought it was me and went out and lifted the car alone, using his knees to help hold the car while someone pulled the child from under the car. I am sure that under normal circumstances he would not have been able to do such a thing. The child was bruised but otherwise all right. Daddy had badly bruised legs, but he too was okay.

On Nancy's sixth birthday, early in April 1943, she had been spending some time with Al's Aunt Bertie and her husband and got a card from Al and Betty, saying they had a surprise for her. Nancy said,

> I told Aunt Bertie, "I'll bet they got married." They had talked about it, and I was excited because most of my friends had mothers, and I wanted one too. That is exactly what they had done, and I was pleased. I was sick a lot at that time. Once before they got married, Mother took me to the doctor, who asked if she was going to marry "this child's father." She said yes, and he told her that I would not live to be ten.

Nancy said she is convinced that she wouldn't have survived childhood if it hadn't been for Betty's care. Chronic illnesses and poor diet after her mother's death were the causes of the doctor's grim prediction about Nancy's prospects. Betty stepped in and helped get Nancy on a path to better health. Years later, Betty was answering questions in one of those memory books people fill out. One of the questions was, "What was your wedding like?" All she said was, "I was scared." When she became pregnant with Judy, the family moved to Dallas. That pregnancy was difficult, and Betty was said to have come close to dying during the delivery. But Judy was a healthy baby, and the family, now four, did pretty well until the end of the war.

After that, things got grim. Al had a hard time competing for work with returning G.I.s, and he tried his hand at several start-up businesses, including tree husbandry. He also had the disadvantage of not being eligible for any benefits from the G.I. Bill. Those were only available to service veterans, not people who had been defense workers. He had another opportunity to rejoin Bob, after the war, but he and Betty were concerned about the amount of traveling Bob was doing by then. Before the war, the band put zillions of miles on their various buses, going out to play jobs on a regular dance circuit—Oklahoma City, Wichita, Fort Smith—and all over the place. But they nearly always came back to Tulsa no matter how far out they'd been that night so they could make their daily radio broadcasts. All of this meant that they traveled a lot but made it back home virtually every night except when they were off making recordings in Dallas or Chicago or on a brief tour of some sort, such as when they went to San Antonio to capitalize on the fame of their hit song "San Antonio Rose." But after the war, Bob was going on more long tours and operating out of California, which made what was already a hard life for musicians and their families even harder. Betty was strongly against it, which Al always said was probably a good decision but which he also had to have regretted later to some degree, given the lousy series of job opportunities he had after the war. Al and Betty left Dallas and moved in with relatives on the family farm in Johnson County, where he tried his hand at budding and grafting pecan trees, which didn't come to much. There wasn't a great demand for that service. He and Betty ran a flower shop for a time, but that didn't work out either. They were just in bad shape financially, and Betty's health hadn't gotten back to normal after Judy's birth. The four of them moved into one room of the old Benton house on the farm with some of the other relatives, with no electricity, no running water in the house, and no indoor plumbing. The effect on Betty was not positive. As Nancy said,

> I'm sure she thought she had come to hell. They were living with folks who were set in their ways. There were pictures of Johnnie everywhere. [Betty] was sick, with a toddler. She probably was thinking, "I thought I was marrying this star. Now I'm down here. We have no money. We have nothing." They were crowded in what had been a log cabin with in-laws who refused to bury a first wife.

In the late 1940s, to pick up some extra income, Al was back playing with bands in and around Fort Worth often at a roadhouse in South Fort Worth called Two Bucks. It was owned by a guy named Buck Russell. I never knew if the name "Two Bucks" meant there was a second "Buck" or if it referred to money. There were tables and a dance floor, a nice place for a night on the town. Not too respectable, but not too shabby. Two of Al's favorite stories came from his time playing at Two Bucks.

One of those stories concerned a guy who was there one night and asking the band to play the "Twelfth Street Rag." He was insistent and got more demanding as he had more to drink. The problem was that the band had been hired to play dance music. That's what people wanted to do at roadhouses, dance, not sit and listen to a crazy-fast novelty tune. Al could play the "Twelfth Street Rag." Most piano players of his era could. But it really was written for a piano player who wanted to show off. No one could have danced to it without risking bodily harm unless it was slowed down—a lot. And that's what the guys in the band finally decided to do. The fellow who kept demanding that they play the song was starting to get on everybody's nerves, including the dancers, so the band tried to play it slowed down. It wasn't much of a dance tune, even at a slower tempo, but they got through it. When they finished, Al asked the man how he liked their version of the "Twelfth Street Rag." He said, "I didn't like it one bit." One of the other guys in the band said, "Well, who are you, and why do you care so much about that song?" The guy said, "I'm Euday Bowman. I wrote the son-of-a-bitch."

The other memorable occurrence from Al's time playing at Two Bucks hearkens back to his relationship with his father, Meeks, and something that had happened to him when Al was in Tulsa with Bob Wills. Everyone who ever knew Al's father said he was a saint if there ever was one. The closest to a curse word anyone ever heard him utter was "frazzlin' on it," which he said once when he hit his head on the edge of a barn door. He was kind, gentle, and thoughtful, and he had a host of admirers. When my sisters would come see him at the farm when they were kids, before they left, he would get them to walk around barefooted in his garden so he could look at their footprints for several days after they went back home. Something he was not proud of was paying a dollar to see a public hanging on the Johnson County courthouse square in Cleburne around 1915. Some enterprising person had gotten control of a good vantage point and was selling spots with a clear view of the proceedings. At the last minute, Meeks turned his head away so he couldn't see the condemned man fall to his death, but he told later of how he thought he shouldn't have been there at all. And he wouldn't any more engage in behavior that his peers at church considered sinful than he would have flapped his arms and flown around his farm. It was well known that Al was a member of the Texas Playboys and well known that they were a dance band. This fact bothered one of the elders at the Church of Christ in Grandview. In Churches of Christ, the congregation is governed by the elders, usually a small number of men, theoretically of good moral standing and sound judgment, though sometimes missing one or another of those virtues as the foibles of human nature slipped in. Meeks happened to be one of the elders at this time, and he became aware that one of the other elders was going around talking to members of the congregation, saying, "You know, Alton is off in Oklahoma in that sinful Texas Playboy band, playing music for dances and no telling what all. I just don't think we ought to have an elder whose son would do something like that." Though Al's work with Bob Wills didn't have anything to do with Meeks, without making a fuss about it or anything, he quietly resigned as an elder and never said a word to anybody about the matter.

Years later, at Two Bucks one night, Al was playing and happened to notice a man and a woman sitting over in a dark corner. He thought he recognized the woman, and then he recognized the man. It was the elder from the church in Grandview who had criticized Meeks for having a son who played in a dance band several years earlier. And here he was, at Two Bucks, with someone else's wife! Al couldn't believe it at first, but then he came to realize it made a lot of sense that this self-righteous guy was out away from home doing something that certainly would get him into trouble with the other elders if it got out. Al decided he just couldn't pass up the opportunity to offer greetings to this fine Christian gentleman and, when the next break came along, he walked over to the booth where the man and woman were sitting. As he approached, he could tell that the man from Grandview recognized him. When Al got to the booth, he just said, "Well, hello, Brother So-and-So. How are you tonight?" The man swallowed hard and just said, "I'm fine, Alton. Just fine." Al knew his father wouldn't have approved of being openly hateful to anyone, even to the man who had tried to shame Meeks by criticizing his son. So he didn't say anything else. But calling the man "Brother," using the language of the church back home, made the point he wanted to make.

After a while, Al and the family managed to get off the farm and rent a house in the Lane Prairie community south of Fort Worth with Betty's sister Ann and her husband, Bill, who had stayed in the service after the war ended and was stationed at Carswell Air Force Base in Fort Worth. It was a step up from a room in the log house, but certainly no palace. The house lacked running water, and after a long dry spell was broken by a nice rain shower, the two families celebrated by bathing the kids outdoors and mopping the floors. Ann and Bill then moved into housing on the base, and because the Stricklins couldn't afford the house by themselves—even with no indoor plumbing—they had to find another place. Then, Al got a job as a traveling furniture salesman. He finally had a good, steady income. They moved to Cleburne and rented a place in the new Jamestown Apartments on North Main Street.

Nancy remembered the move to Cleburne as a disaster in some ways, at least for Betty. As on the farm, there were reminders of Johnnie everywhere, especially among people who remembered her fondly and hadn't been around Al or Nancy at the time of Johnnie's death back in Tulsa. Betty was seeing a couple of doctors in Fort Worth, and she started taking some strong prescriptions to help with her physical difficulties. Then, on a visit to a park, she fell from a low tree branch she was sitting on and broke her coccyx. Al always described that injury as a major downturn in Betty's health, more so even than the difficult delivery of Judy. He always said she had been more fun-loving before these things happened. Afterward, she had what people then called "nervous problems" and relied on prescription pain relievers. She never drank much alcohol. Neither of them did. Al could put away impressive amounts of beer when he was fishing or shucking corn on the cob, but I never saw him inebriated. And it would be going too far to say Betty was addicted to pills, but she always had a doctor in those days who was willing to prescribe her something. Her health problems made her life a lot less pleasant than it would have been without them and had a big impact on the rest of the family. I think a lot of people neglected to see the basic unhappiness at the bottom of a lot of her problems. Medicine didn't have much to offer in alleviating that. What was needed was the possibility of better times and better moods.

Bob Wills and His Texas Playboys at Cain's in Tulsa in 1937, with Al seated at the piano (center). Photo courtesy of the Estate of Bob Wills and the Oklahoma Historical Society.

Al and his first wife, Arbutus (Johnnie) Watson Stricklin.

Al with his new daughter, Nancy Jo Stricklin, and his mother, Annie, and Annie's mother, Bettie Bascom Benton, 1937.

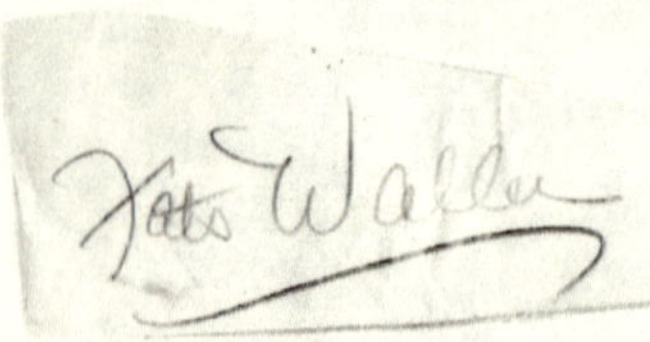

Autograph of Fats Waller, one of Al's heroes, from his scrapbook.

Johnnie and Nancy just before Johnnie's illness set in.

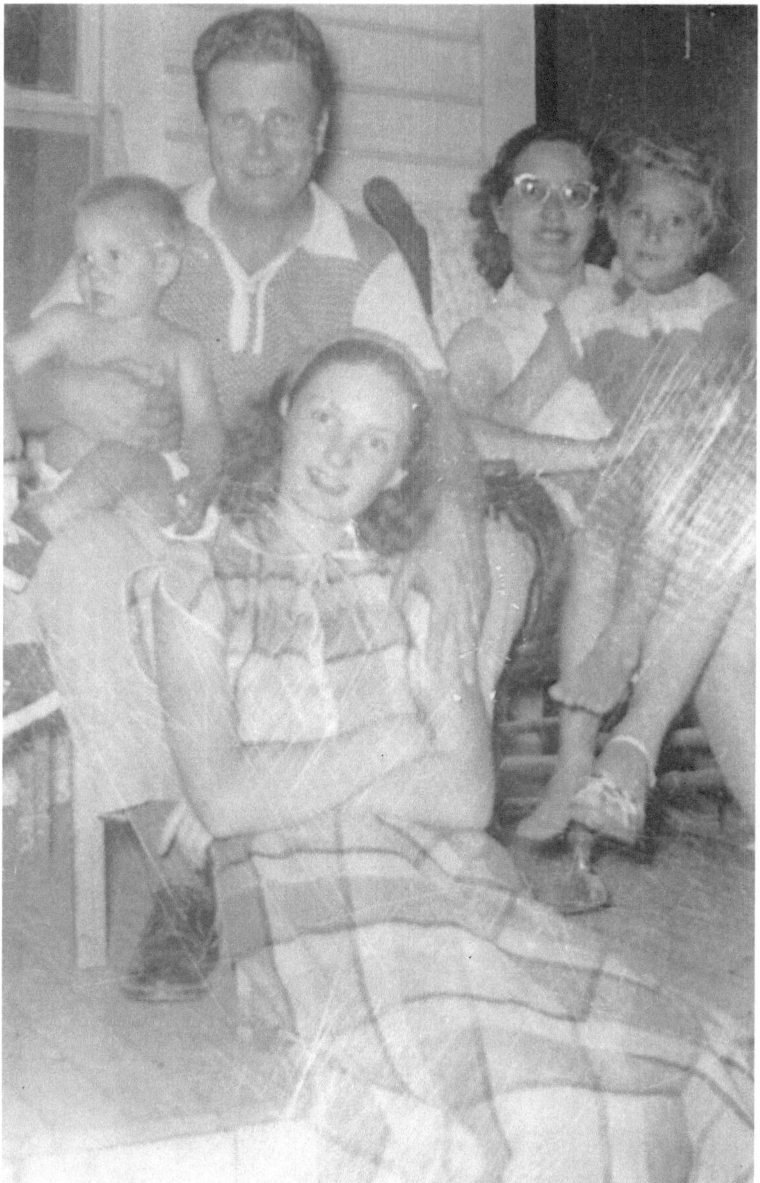

Al and Betty with Nancy, front, and David and Judy.

Al and Betty shortly after their marriage.

Al when he was manager of the piano and organ department at McCord Music in Dallas.

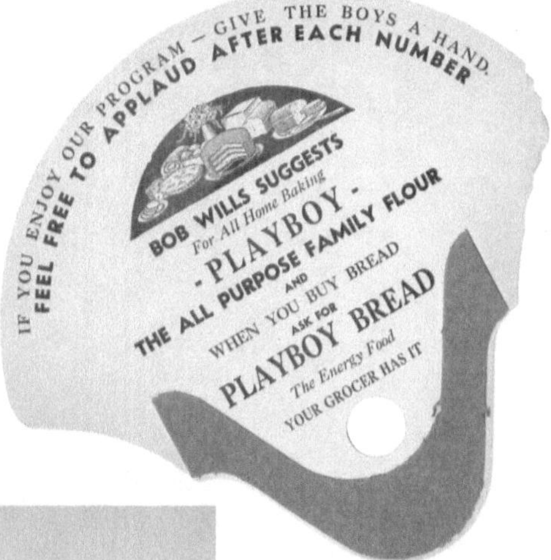

Fan handed out at live broadcasts, promoting flour and bread deals made by the Bob Wills organization.

Betty Jo Zeigler in 1940, before she and Al met.

Al and daughter Judy playing in the backyard of the house in Cleburne.

Al when he was broadcasting "Bargains with Music" for Dickson's Furniture and Appliance over KCLE in Cleburne.

Al during his ill-fated pecan business, with Betty and his father, Meeks, in back, and Benton and Violet, his brother and sister, in front.

Al and Betty just before the Original Texas Playboys reunited.

Betty when she was keeping books for Colquit-Lacewell Drug Company in Cleburne.

CHAPTER 7

New Start

In 1950, and for a time, things started looking up. Al got a job working for a Cleburne businessman named Fred Dickson, who owned several large buildings downtown just east of the Johnson County courthouse square and who sold home furnishings and, importantly for Al, pianos and organs. Al quickly showed a talent for marketing and promotions that he had never had a chance to demonstrate before. Nancy remembered that he hired a woman to sleep in a bed in the store's show window for one promotion and, despite their normal nine o'clock opening time, wouldn't unlock the doors the next morning until eleven. Customers were lined up for a city block, she said. He would offer to sell people an entire house full of furniture at one time, which might have been done somewhere else but seemed unusual in Cleburne.

Then he started doing a half-hour remote broadcast over the local radio station, KCLE. The show aired for several years during the late 1950s and early '60s and was called "Bargains with Music." He broadcast live from one of the show windows in the music department of Dickson's, looking out onto Henderson Street, the main east-west route through Cleburne in those days and part of U.S. Highway 67.

No matter the weather, he always began the show by saying, "It's a beautiful day in Cleburne!" Then he would play a song and talk about the bargains you could get on pianos and organs at Dickson's, as well as furniture, appliances, and the like. He told stories about growing up in Johnson County and going off to play with the Texas Playboys, and people got where they would drive by the store when they knew Al was doing the show. They'd wave and sometimes honk their horns, hoping Al would say something about them. A lot of the songs he played, of course, were pop standards. Years later, when Al met Willie Nelson for the first time, Willie told him he used to listen to that show when he would come visit relatives in Cleburne and first heard some of the classic American pop tunes of the twentieth century on "Bargains with Music." Some of those songs ended up on Willie's 1978 album *Stardust.*

Along with the money Betty was making at a job she got at the local Ford dealership, Al's salary was good enough that in 1950 they were able to build a house on West Fifth Street, a side street in a quiet neighborhood southwest of downtown Cleburne. The home on Fifth Street was a modest three-bedroom frame house. Most of the houses on Forest and Prairie and the other big streets nearby were larger and somewhat fancier than the houses on the numbered streets. But Al and Betty were proud that they were able to put together the financing necessary to build a house that cost twelve thousand dollars. They hoped it would be the turning point toward a more prosperous future. An alley ran beside the house and behind the houses that fronted Forest Avenue, and this alley became the main thoroughfare for neighborhood kids. After a few years, one of the mothers, Florence Baker, dubbed our gang of ten or twelve kids the "Alley Rats." The main park in Cleburne was a five-minute walk away. Fairly good-sized creeks ran along the neighborhood to the east and to the west. It was a great place to bring up children, and there were plenty of us. So many babies were born in a three-year period within about a five-block area that people around town referred to our neighborhood as the Fertile Crescent. We were living in one of the prime sectors of the Baby Boom. And it was an unusually diverse neighborhood religiously. In addition to the usual Texas cross-section of Baptists, Church of Christ folks, Methodists, and Presbyterians, there were two Catholic families, a Mormon family, and a Jewish family. Also, Cleburne had a very interesting collection of town characters. One was a woman everybody called the Dog Lady. She lived next to the town dump and had what seemed like two dozen dogs, which she led around on occasion. Everybody said she was a millionaire who had her money stashed around the shack she lived in. Then there was a man who sold hot tamales out of a box he had rigged up on the handlebars of a bicycle. There were lots of stories about fortune telling and seances and other weird stuff going on at his house, where the tamales were cooked. There was another constant bike rider the kids called Ring Ring, which is what he said when he saw people as he made his rounds. There were others, as I'm sure there were and are in other small towns, but I don't know of anybody who ever tried to ask these folks about their lives. They probably had some interesting stories!

Nancy said about the new house,

> That was one of the most exciting things that had ever happened to us. It was great fun to watch the house go up. David was born after we built the house, and that was quite an event. I thought he belonged to me, just as Judy did. In fact, Mother was sick much of the time, and he was mine to care for. Sometimes I would find her passed out on the floor. And when she had bad headaches, she would darken the room, close the bedroom door, and we knew to leave her alone.

As traumatic as that kind of occurrence was, the family's financial situation was improving, with Al's job at Dickson's and Betty's work, which she was nearly always able to get to in those days. Then Al decided to start his own business selling home furnishings and the like and had a disastrous experience with a partner who embezzled money from the firm. By now, Nancy was old enough to work and was keeping the books. She discovered what was going on but couldn't convince Al that his partner was a crook until it was too late. Al and Betty got left holding the debts. Efforts by their lawyer to get the vanished partner back to face his bad behavior came to nothing. They had greater debts than the value of their assets, but every discussion about declaring bankruptcy ended with a "no." Al and Betty both had a horror of bankruptcy. They thought people ought to make good on what they owed. Declaring bankruptcy might have been an easier way out of the trouble they found themselves in, but they thought it was dishonorable and wouldn't do it. They also refused to press charges against the former partner. Al got back on with Dickson's, after some anxious negotiations, and they paid off their debts from the failed business. It was a tense time, though. Nancy said she was riding with them one time and got so sick of the argument they were having that she made them stop the car and threatened to get out and ride a bus home. Nancy and Judy asked me once if I remembered any of the events from this period. I said, "I remember the yelling." Al never talked much about the failed business, but years later I noticed that he would never buy gas at a Gulf station. He'd drive by a Gulf station with cheaper gas to go to one with a different brand. I finally asked him why, and he told me that his former business partner had run up a sizeable bill with Gulf and that the company was not very pleasant about how long he took to pay off the debt. He said he'd never buy anything from them again.

It wasn't all unhappiness, by any means. Some crazy things happened in the house on West Fifth Street, including the time Judy and our cousin Billy, Aunt Ann and Uncle Bill's son, had a Roman candle fight—in the kitchen. They were both about ten years old and figured out how to light the fireworks on the gas stove. The grownups didn't think much of that activity, but it provided a fun story. Al loved fireworks and always made sure we had a bunch of them around the Fourth of July and Christmas so we could shoot them in the street in front of the house. That was probably illegal, but it was fun. People came over to the house and danced on the hardwood floor in the living room, where Aunt Violet's old piano stood and where Al entertained guests. He nearly always created an atmosphere of joy. Nancy and Judy describe him as more of a companion than a parent and especially recall his great bedtime stories. Judy said,

> It was normal for him to crawl into a little kid's pool with me and splash around, play with the toys, and make faces at the camera pointed at us. He also told the most incredible bedtime stories. Never a tired old story, always a fresh new tale of nonsense and exaggerated feats. The heroes in his stories were normal folks, but able to do anything at any time and with great flair.

Judy also recalled her habit of sneaking around the house, looking for interesting items our parents had stashed away:

> His closet was often the scene of my snooping crimes, for it held wondrous goodies. Old seventy-eight RPM records, most of them in album-type covers, were of great interest to me. Many were records of Bob Wills, Bing Crosby, Glenn Miller, etc. I would sneak a stack of

> records out of the closet and start listening to them, and one or both of my parents would suddenly appear in the room. Mother would want to show me dance steps to the music, and Daddy would want to tell me how good the music was "back in those days." There were also stacks of picture albums. I'd never seen most of the people in the pictures. I'd also never seen my parents looking as happy as they always did in those shots. Many were of my parents and the same group of friends who were out fishing, hiking, canoeing, and just laughing together. I later learned most of those outings took place around the time World War II broke out, the last time some of those guys were ever around for a good while.

Betty loved music and nearly always had something going on the record player. One of her favorite outings was a time, years later, when we took her to see the Mills Brothers at the Adolphus Hotel in Dallas. When the great trio came down off the stage and passed near the table where we were sitting, she jumped up to tell them how wonderful she thought they were. The emcee had asked the crowd to stay seated while they left, but she couldn't contain herself, startling the three brothers, one of whom, it turned out, was blind. She loved to dance, in the living room or anywhere she had the chance. Betty and Al told jokes and crazy stories when company came over. There was a lot of laughing on those occasions. And they were welcoming to Nancy's boyfriend, a young electrician named Jerry Willis, who had moved up from Galveston to work at the huge Santa Fe Railroad diesel-engine maintenance and repair shops in Cleburne. He became a welcome addition to the family, though there are stories about how I would wedge myself between Jerry and Nancy when they were trying to sit together on the living room couch, saying, "You stay away from my Sissy Jo!" They got married in that living room in 1956, my earliest memory. Years later, Jerry earned Stricklin-family immortality by nicknaming Betty "Sweet Thing."

Jerry figured in an episode that demonstrated Al's comic timing and his awareness that saying a little can be a lot funnier than saying a lot, also that pretending to be dignified while doing something ridiculous can be even funnier. The episode also connected with what Judy called Al's "obsession with yard work." As she put it, "He could get anything to grow and took great delight in tending to his yard and his gardens." She added, "He hated water rationing that took place in the summers when the city was suffering from droughts, and he would go to great lengths to find ways to water his lawn, even if that meant watering from 10 p.m. until 5 a.m." All of these factors came together when Nancy and then-boyfriend Jerry came back from a date late one night and were saying goodnight on the front steps of the house on Fifth Street. What they didn't know was that Al had just gone out into the night to move the water sprinkler. It was summer, and the sprinkler was the only hope for the St. Augustine grass he was so proud of. Unbeknownst to Nancy and Jerry, Al was out in the yard in his boxer shorts. Because we lived on a side street, there were very few cars out and about after ten o'clock, and Al didn't want to take the time to put on some trousers just to run out into the dark and move the sprinkler. He was awfully hot-natured anyway, so stripping down to as little as possible fit his plan for staying cool. He had been around on the side of the house when Nancy and Jerry got home, and he thought he'd just wait them out. It wouldn't quite do to walk up out of the darkness in his underwear and scare the boyfriend to death. But the wait turned into quite a long time. Amazingly, hot-natured Al started to get a little chilled, and he remembered seeing some sheets hanging on the clothesline in the backyard. This was back when Betty was still able to do such chores as hanging clothes on the line, and she hadn't gone back out to get them at the end of the daylight. Al went into the backyard and got one of the sheets, wrapped it around himself, and, with all the dignity he could muster, came walking up the steps, and just said, "Pardon me." Nancy and Jerry were too stunned to say anything as they let him pass between them and go into the house. The next morning, Betty said, "The strangest thing happened last night. Someone got in the backyard and stole just one sheet."

Jerry had moved to Cleburne soon after graduating from Galveston's Ball High School to do an apprenticeship as an electrician at the gigantic Santa Fe facility. For a period of about a hundred years, working at "the Santa Fe shops" was one of the main things people in Cleburne did. Jerry's parents gave him twenty dollars and the name of someone to talk to at the shops about a job and put him on the train in Galveston. He got the job in Cleburne, and soon he met Nancy. They dated for a year or so and then got married. After a couple of years, Jerry decided to join the Coast Guard. Even though the conflict in Vietnam wasn't yet to the point where it involved vast numbers of U.S. service personnel, the Cold War–era draft was very much a factor in young men's minds, and Jerry thought he might end up being stationed closer to home if he was in the Coast Guard. He was exactly right. While he was being processed in New Orleans, it became known that he was an electrician. The Coast Guard needed an electrician in Galveston, and so his first assignment was in his hometown. Nancy gave birth to their first child, Leigh Anne, there in April 1959. Jerry and Nancy were living in a garage apartment then, not too far from Jerry's parents' house, which was just a few minutes' walk from the famous Galveston Sea

Wall. The deadly hurricane and tidal wave of 1900 were still vivid memories for some of the older residents, and hurricane preparedness was a big deal, but this was before the advances in weather forecasting that help people get ready for big storms today. So, when Betty, Judy, and I rode the train to Galveston to see the new baby in July, we didn't realize we were going to be there when Hurricane Debra hit. Al had needed to stay in Cleburne a few extra days and planned to follow us down in the car to see Leigh Anne, visit for a few days, and drive us back home.

When the storm hit, we all had to hunker down at the home of Jerry's parents, whose house was close to the beach but situated on the side of a hill that protected it, to a great extent, from high winds and flooding. Jerry's dad hung the storm shutters, and we waited out the hurricane. Al wasn't supposed to come down for a few more days, but he couldn't get us on the phone and couldn't stand not knowing how we were. So he decided to drive on down to Galveston. He set out in our '56 Pontiac and made it close to the coast while the storm was still raging. He got stopped by highway patrol officers at the top of a hill. They told him once he drove down the other side he'd be driving in water, and they couldn't guarantee his safety. He insisted on trying to make it and headed slowly down the hill. Water got into the interior of the car and started gathering in the floorboard. At one point his right foot was completely underwater while pressing on the accelerator. But he made it to the other side of the low spot he was driving through, stopped for a minute to collect himself and make sure the car's engine wasn't going to stall, and then he saw that there were hundreds, maybe thousands, of snakes on the road. They had fled the rising water. It was very creepy, but he did the only thing he could do, which was drive. By the time he got to Galveston Island, the storm had moved enough that the police let him in. We were shocked when he got to us. We had no idea he was even trying to get down there.

Judy recalled how Al conducted himself at holidays and religious events, sometimes seriously and sometimes not so much:

> I loved holidays with my family. We weren't the kind of family that went to Christmas Eve services or prayed on a daily basis. But come Thanksgiving, Christmas Day, Easter Sunday, etc., the relatives would come out of the woodwork for a gathering. It was during these times that I came to witness people coming together and enjoying the stories of those no longer with us, how our family came to Texas and such. I also would hear my father lead us in prayer. I wondered why we prayed at holiday meals but no other times. Maybe being with the entire family brought out the gratitude in him. The only other times I remember him praying were at church when he'd serve communion or be asked to give the closing prayer. I was always slightly nervous about that because he had usually been the cause of my laughing during a song or during the sermon. I always held my breath and hoped he didn't start laughing during the prayer. He had this habit of uttering the word "buff." It was kind of a word he substituted for "hi" or "excuse me" or various other phrases. I don't know when this word entered his vocabulary or why, but hearing him say "buff" in the middle of a really serious moment could just get me laughing.

One of the lines Al often uttered after a big holiday meal was, "I wonder what the poor folks are doing?" We always laughed at that because we certainly were not rich, but probably also because, by the time he took to saying that, we weren't actually poor. His sense of humor and sometimes crazy behavior went in another direction, too, as Judy recalled:

The other thing that would make all of us laugh was for him to refer to passing gas as "stepping on frogs." This did not amuse our mother. He would stroll down the hallway in his boxer shorts, walk through her bedroom on the way to the kitchen, mumbling "buff" to anyone in the room, and let one go. This was immediately followed by "Oops, somebody stepped on a frog." I think he did this partly for the attention he'd receive from those of us who would laugh and partly to get a disgusted reaction from his wife.

At some point, Al told us about a classification system for examples of that particular activity, stepping on frogs, that members of the Texas Playboys developed during the long hours traveling to shows and dances. The guys rode in a bus while Bob rode in his car, so Bob was never around to witness the full effects of long hours, strange eating and drinking habits, and sheer boredom that inspired the creation of their system, which fell into three groups based on sound quality and volume:

Fizz
Fuzz
Fizz Fuzz
Fizz Fuzz Buzz

Poot
Tatter-poot

Fart
Buck Fart
Tear Ass
Rattler

We thought that was all pretty amazing, and when Al's grandkids got old enough to learn of these mysteries, they were thrilled, as were their kids, to memorize the system and talk about it at every opportunity. It all made sense, given the fact that the Texas Playboys were all obsessed with sound.

Judy had some other, less pungent memories about holidays:

> An event that always took place a couple of weeks after Thanksgiving was always puzzling to me. He'd take me with him to do his Christmas shopping for Mother. I'd jump in the car and start talking to him about all kinds of things we might get for her. My ideas were never very good, but he never needed them anyway. We'd end up at the one department store in town, and I would help him choose from an array of clothing that Mother had previously picked out and put on hold so he would give her an appropriate gift. I guess she and Daddy worked out a system with the store so she'd at least get something she would enjoy.
>
> We also enjoyed a Christmas Eve ritual together. After my little brother had fallen asleep, we would tear into the boxes of things such as army or western town sets that needed assembling. I was better at using the screwdriver and pliers than he was, but I think he had as much fun playing with the sets as I did. He also gobbled up the cookies and milk that David and I had set out for Santa. I, of course, was old enough to be able to watch that, but young enough to hope that maybe another Santa would come by after I'd gone to bed.

For much of the 1950s and '60s, Betty was able to work, usually doing bookkeeping in places such as the Colquitt-Lacewell Drugstore in downtown Cleburne. The majority of mothers didn't work outside the home, so Betty was a little unusual for our neighborhood. Most of the dads worked in businesses and offices in

Cleburne. Because Al was forty-four when I was born, he was older than the fathers of my friends, and he didn't pal around much with them. Most of them were World War II veterans. One had been seriously wounded on D-Day and was said to have a piece of shrapnel still in his neck. The dad from the Jewish family had also fought in Europe and had been taken prisoner by the Germans. There were whispers about the torments he probably experienced in a Nazi POW camp. Al never talked about the fact that he hadn't been in the service but had done defense work instead, but I thought it might have been the reason he didn't feel close to the men in our neighborhood. But he was regarded as a friendly, helpful fellow who was a good neighbor. He could be impatient, especially with himself, and he could be awfully pessimistic, seeing patterns in bad news. But some of the neighborhood kids loved to come over for his famous Stricklin Burgers and hear his funny stories. He kept the lawn mowed, the place picked up, and the house painted, and he rooted for the home team and did all the other things expected of a "head of the house" in those days. A lot of people knew he was a gifted piano player, but everybody knew he was a nice man and fun to be around. Nancy's daughter, Leigh Anne, said that when she was with him, she was convinced she was his favorite grandchild, and she learned later that Pete and Robert, her brothers, had the same feeling. He made each of them feel special.

Al played the piano at meetings of civic and service organizations, school events, and retail promotions. There's a photo of him that includes a little kid—who looks a lot like a ten-year-old me—standing next to the piano Al is playing, on a trailer in the street on the courthouse square in Cleburne, probably as part of a Chamber of Commerce event or something similar. The parents of our generation probably knew who Bob Wills was and might have known that Al had been in his band. But kids? Not much of a chance. We were being bombarded with Little Richard and Elvis and Buddy Holly, the dozens of doo-wop groups, and then the urban folk revival and the British Invasion. Not many young people were paying a lot of attention to western swing in those days. As a matter of fact, the same could be said for adults. Al's full-time membership in Bob's band had ended only twenty or twenty-five years earlier, and Bob was still making music until he had his first stroke in 1969. But Al's identity around Cleburne was focused more on being a guy with a day job who really could "tear up" a piano.

From the time that I was a little kid, I always knew he had been a full-time musician earlier in his life. In the first place, there were these records. I don't remember a time when we put them on and listened to them as a family. I often put them on the turntable and listened to them by myself, but I don't remember ever sitting down with him in those days and playing the old recordings and asking him about them. But because I grew up listening to recordings from his time in the band and because Bob Wills never failed to call out his name when he played a solo, I learned from an early age to listen to those songs so I could hear the man with the enthusiastic voice say my father's name. One funny thing happened when I was little and listening to Bob's recording of "Roly Poly." This recording was made after Al left the band, but I liked it anyway. It was about a chubby kid who had a big appetite and a lot of energy, which he expended while doing chores and running around all over town. The refrain went, "Roly Poly, Daddy's little fatty. Bet he's gonna be a man someday." When Tommy Duncan sang "Daddy's little fatty," it seemed to me that he put a little extra syllable in there so it sounded like "Daddy's *a* little fatty." Al was always trying to lose weight in those days, so that seemed to make some sense. But the other part I took to be "Betty's gonna be a man someday." Given the fact that that was my mother's name, I pondered that one for a time.

In those days, just about every adult smoked cigarettes. In fact, they smoked just about everywhere, just about all the time. Betty smoked Viceroys. Al smoked Camels until the mid-1960s and tried several times to quit. This was before U.S. health agencies started issuing warnings about cigarettes, but he decided he wanted to quit anyway. For several months he carried a pack of Camels around in his shirt pocket. Every now and then, he'd pull the pack out and give the cigarettes what a friend of ours would have called a "dog-cussing." That was his way of dealing with his craving for nicotine. He tried smoking cigars for a while, even a pipe, but he finally figured he just needed to get out of the tobacco business altogether. Betty was a different story. She finally managed to quit, but only after many more years and after doing terrible damage to her respiratory system and heart. I hated being around them when they were smoking, so whatever lectures anybody might have had to offer me about the ills of smoking were unnecessary, which was also true of my sisters. Smoking was at the heart of one of Betty's funniest moments, though.

We had gone to the state park west of Cleburne and rented a little boat to take a trip around the lake in the center of the park. Betty was never a fan of the outdoors. We went on a total of about one picnic in the whole history of our family, and never a walk, let alone a hike. She thought of the outdoors as that unpleasant space you had to pass through to get from your air-conditioned house to your air-conditioned car and then to the store or the place where you worked. Amazingly enough, on this occasion we managed to talk her into going to Cleburne State Park. We were having a good visit until we decided to get into the boat. As Betty was trying to step into it, she lost her footing and went right into the water. Every part of her went under except the hand that was holding her lit cigarette. The water was cold, and it must have been quite a shock. As soon as her head came up out of that water, she took a drag on her Viceroy, standing shoulder deep in the lake. The only serious damage was a broken fingernail, but the experience didn't gain any points for the great outdoors.

Smoking also created a bit of a memorable debate I had with Betty. She was telling me one time about how bad smoking was for you, while smoking a cigarette. I made a crack about how that might be a little ironic. I don't think I said "hypocritical," but she said, as she did on many occasions, "Do as I say, not as I do." I used to kid her that that was her motto. But I didn't really think of her as a hypocrite, and I would even say that she had a highly developed sense of ethics, something Al always said he admired about her. His way of saying it was that she was a "good woman," by which I always thought he meant someone who had standards and tried to live up to them. One of the things she would have included as evidence was staying committed to their marriage. All five of her siblings had been divorced at least once, but she was determined to break that pattern. I once heard her tell someone who was talking about the number of divorces in their family, "We don't do that in this family." Betty knew there were people who needed out of bad marriages, but she just didn't want to think that would come to pass in hers. So she made sure it didn't.

I have a tiny handful of memories of seeing Al and Betty having a conversation. I never thought of them as particularly affectionate toward one another, and, in many ways, they lived separate lives. When I was a little, I once asked Betty why so many songs were about love. She answered, without any hesitation, "Because it's the most wonderful thing there is." I remember wondering how she knew that. There didn't seem to be much evidence of romantic love in her life. Most of their conversations seemed to have to do with the regular, run-of-the-mill topics: paying their bills, getting other household business taken care of, and making sure the place was in reasonably good shape. Sometimes I thought some of Betty's concerns about those things came from her desire to maintain, or develop, something of a classy appearance. Betty and Al had every expectation that my sisters and I would be good citizens and contribute to the community. To some, this concern with appearances might have seemed out of place in a family so tied to the entertainment business, which often seemed to attract people who didn't care at all about how people saw them as long as they bought their records or went to see their movies. I think Al's part of that originated to a great degree with his family upbringing and got reinforced by his association with Bob Wills, who wanted his band members to be well regarded, both as good musicians and as people folks would enjoy having as neighbors. He told me that once a man had asked if he'd shown him pictures of his grandchildren, and he responded, "No, and I sure do appreciate it!" I told him, "You didn't say that to that guy!" And he admitted he hadn't but that he had thought about it. He never would have done something that rude.

Neither Betty nor Al grew up having any money, but Betty's upbringing had been much more precarious than Al's. My sisters and I are convinced that she was marked by that for the rest of her life. Her actions and opinions probably did reflect a concern about "keeping up with the Joneses." Mostly, though, the Stricklins simply wanted to be good neighbors and good members of the community, in whatever ways they could. Betty was in the King's Daughters and was even in a bowling league for a time, before her health caved in. Al never joined a civic club or other organization, but he provided entertainment for countless events and meetings. They both stayed in the Church of Christ for the rest of their lives. They tried to exhibit the qualities they valued in the relationships they maintained around town and beyond.

Al and Betty enjoyed playing bridge, which was a very popular card game among both men and women in those days. And they did a lot with their friends Lee and Evelyn Ponder, who were really interesting people. Lee had been in Jimmy Doolittle's unit during World War II and was supposed to make the famous 1942 "Thirty Seconds Over Tokyo" bombing raid but got bumped at the last minute in favor of the crew member who saved Captain Ted Lawson's life by amputating his badly damaged leg. The Ponders had a myna named Ponderosa, which could mimic speech and other sounds. Lee taught it fractured versions of poems and speeches, including an alternate version of the first lines of the Gettysburg Address, "Four score and twenty years ago . . ." which the bird would do in Lee's West Texas accent. Evelyn had a very strong South Carolina accent, and Ponderosa would mimic her by saying, "I believe I'll have a glass of water," with "waw-ta" sounding like someone from *Cat on a Hot Tin Roof.* The two couples had a lot of laughter-filled get-togethers. I got to tag along on some of those visits to Lee and Evelyn's house and hang around when the Ponders came over to our house. Al would play the piano, and they all would talk into the night.

Al's close friends tended to be men he'd known earlier in his life. He kept in touch with the great Playboy vocalist Tommy Duncan, who grew up not far from Cleburne and who came to see Al from time to time. Al stayed in touch with Smoky Dacus, his old buddy from the rhythm section of the Playboys. Because they were so central to the success of the rhythm section, which was the driving force of the Texas Playboy sound, Smoky and Al always had a special bond. Al also kept in touch with a Dallas friend named Wylie St. Claire, who had a rambunctious dog named Max that Wylie sometimes admonished by saying, "Down, Max, lest I strike thee," which Al thought was hilarious. Wylie had been in a band starting in the 1920s called the Joy Stompers, which he and Al enjoyed talking about. Al also stayed close to a couple of Austin friends, both lawyers, his old friend Manley Head, the guy who went with Al on the 1926 adventure to the Rio Grande Valley and with us to the Asleep at the Wheel show at the Ritz Theater in 1974, and Jerry Prestridge, who had grown up in Johnson County and taken some piano lessons from Al when he was a kid. Al also kept in touch with Larry White, his old bandmate from KFJZ days, whose nickname was Yoyo and who was a character with a quick wit and a crazy story. Larry was especially fond of making odd orders in cafes. He and Al would go someplace to eat, and Larry would order raw liver and onions, which would throw the server into a tizzy. Eventually, Larry would back off and order something normal. But he might follow the request for raw liver and onions with one for a "mad-duck sandwich." When the server asked what that was, Larry would say, "Don't you know how to make a duck mad? You goose it. And do you know how to make a goose mad? You duck it!" This was exactly the kind of corny humor they used between songs when they were playing on the radio. Al always thought Larry could have been a successful comedian if he'd gotten a couple of breaks, though he did say he knew there was only so far you could go with humor based on stories about mad ducks and geese.

Al's friend Manley Head played something of a role in a scary episode, our experience of the Cuban missile crisis in fall 1962, which showed Al's serious side. Al talked very often about the Cold War and the race with the Soviets, including their launch of Sputnik in 1957. We didn't know anything then about satellites and imagined Sputnik was a giant space fortress ready to rain destruction down on the United States. We later found out it was about the size of a washing machine. A few years later, when the United States really got going in its space race with the Soviet Union, Al and I would watch the television coverage of the U.S. space flights early in the mornings before the school and work days began. Sometimes during launch delays, which were frequent, he'd argue with Betty to let me stay home from school to watch the broadcasts on the basis that "this is history being made." When the Cuban Missile Crisis gripped the nation in October 1962, we were right there with it.

This was one of the most interesting events, to me, in my family's history. Everybody always thought of Betty as the worrier. She drove my sisters and me crazy fretting about everything. As I got close to draft age in the last years of the Vietnam War, she told me if I got drafted, she'd knock me on the head, throw me in the trunk of her car, and drive me to Canada. That turned out not to be necessary, but I thought she might be capable of something very much like that. If my sisters or I ever came in late, we usually had to wait up even later for Al to get back from driving around town, which Betty had sent him to do, checking the hospital to see if we'd been brought in or ditches alongside roads in the area if the ambulance hadn't found us yet. He often told me that my mother was a lot like his mother in this respect, always worrying, usually needlessly. Al was always considered more laid-back than Betty, and he usually was. Of course, what I never let on was that some of those out-too-late episodes actually were perilous, especially when my friend William Daniel and I were loose on his family's ranch. I accumulated several near-death experiences in William's company, all carefully unmentioned in Betty's presence. But during the missile crisis, Al sprang into action because he was genuinely worried about Nancy, Judy, and me, as countless parents were.

Because Nancy's husband, Jerry, was in the Coast Guard, everybody in the family was terrified that he would get pulled into the conflict and be in terrible danger. Al got in touch with Manley to see if he could use his contacts with Lyndon Johnson and other Texas Democrats, who in those days wielded a lot of influence in Washington, and get Jerry disconnected from any duty that would involve messing with the Soviets. Al later realized he had put Manley in an awkward spot and said he knew that's not the way the military works, fielding calls from anxious fathers-in-law trying to get service personnel away from possible danger. But the episode showed his concern for his son-in-law and his confidence that his old friend could help.

Jerry's Coast Guard service wasn't the only source of anxiety, though. Judy had gone off to college in Denton just weeks before, and Al and Betty talked a lot about whether they should go get her. Both were anxious, but Al got my attention because his behavior was so much more dramatic than usual. He talked a lot about how close Cleburne was to Carswell Air Force Base in Fort Worth, a Strategic Air Command facility with nuclear-armed B-52s whose around-the-clock flights had long since become commonplace in the lives of everybody who lived near Fort Worth. Part of his conversation about Carswell was colored by the fact that he knew a fair bit about the place because Uncle Bill, Betty's brother-in-law, had been stationed there during his service in the Air Force and had told Al about the base during the time the two families were living together in the late '40s. We studied the articles in the *Fort Worth Star-Telegram*, with their charts and maps showing the expected levels of damage within the immediate blast radius and each five-mile increment beyond that. We determined that Cleburne was in for a bad time if Soviet missiles launched from Cuba hit Carswell, which everybody expected they surely would do. We loaded up on canned goods, planned where we would go in the house in case of a nuclear attack, and agreed on a route I would use to walk home from elementary school in case of an alert. There were four or five variations on my usual route walking home, one involving wading through a creek, but we fixed the one route I was supposed to take so Al and Betty would know where to find me if they had to race home from work and pick me up along the way. Then we would all hunker down and await the blast or the fires or the fallout. It was a scary couple of weeks, and then it was over.

Al's pessimistic side showed up in seemingly insignificant ways. One was his almost perpetual state of agitation about the weather. If the weather forecast called for a thirty percent chance of rain anywhere near Cleburne, he was personally offended if it didn't rain on our yard and his garden. It was useless to point out that a thirty percent chance of rain probably meant a seventy percent chance of no rain. Also, he hated getting stopped by red lights and always took it personally when a stoplight would turn red as he approached an intersection. Of course, he didn't notice all the times when he had green lights. He only remembered the red ones. He would take a route where he knew there were several, maybe many, stop signs to avoid the possibility, just the possibility, of getting stopped by a red light and dealing with that disappointment. Getting delayed in traffic just drove him nuts. If we ever had to wait for a bunch of cars to go past, he would say, "Come on, all million of you!" But one funny story came of all this pessimism. We were going out to visit someone at the hospital, which then was on North Main Street in Cleburne. Instead of driving on Main—possible red lights!—we were on a side street with what seemed to me ten stop signs. He didn't care about that. But then at one of the intersections, a four-way stop, we stopped opposite a pickup truck. The driver must have dropped something and gotten down on the floorboard to pick it up, and the pickup was just sitting at the south-facing stop sign as we went past it, heading north. When we went through the intersection we looked over at the pickup. The driver had a big dog riding in the cab, and while the driver was bent down toward the floorboard the dog jumped up on the seat and put its paws on the steering wheel, which made it look like the dog was driving the pickup. Without missing a beat, Al just said, "Well, that's something you don't see every day."

Betty and Al weren't much for vacations, in part, because they never had jobs that gave them any paid time off. If they went anywhere, it was usually to see her family in northeastern Oklahoma, though a couple of times we went to see some transplanted Oklahoma friends, the Jacksons, who then lived in Corpus Christi. We would go to Paris, Texas, where Al's brother and sister-in-law, Benton and Hazel, lived. We went to San Marcos and San Antonio once on an actual vacation and saw the mermaids at Aquarena Springs and toured the Alamo. Betty and Al had some friends who had a place—actually, a mobile home—in Ruidoso, New Mexico, and we went up there several summers, along with every other Texan who wanted to escape the heat and see the horse races at Ruidoso Downs. But most trips involved going to Hominy, where Betty's mother and aunt lived, and to other nearby towns where

Zeigler kin lived. Betty had a friend who worked for an oil company in an office building in Bartlesville, and he took us to see their computer, which was about the size of a school bus. Betty was particularly impressed, having spent so much of her work life operating adding machines and posting transaction entries by hand. But most of the visits to her family involved sitting around and talking, lots of loud talking, and lots of smoking and drinking.

It never occurred to me till decades later that when we were in Oklahoma, we never went to Tulsa or even just drove by Cain's, though it was then, as it still is, an active music venue. Al had so many important experiences there that you might have thought he would want to drive around Tulsa and show us the sights. A somewhat similar thing, with one important difference, happened when he got a job in Dallas in the early 1960s, which turned out to be just a few blocks from the old warehouse at 508 Park where the Texas Playboys made their first recordings in September 1935. I think Al would have driven me by the place if he'd known it was still standing. This was, after all, less than thirty years after those recordings were made. But I think he didn't do that because that warehouse hadn't made much of an impression on him. In his stories about that recording session, he always talked about how hot it was, how hard some guys worked to get a piano up on the floor where they made the recordings, how funny it was to watch the refined Englishman Art Satherley interact with Bob Wills and His Texas Playboys, but not much about the building and what part of town it was in. In the early 1960s, 508 Park wasn't as well-known as it later became after Eric Clapton went there to record a tribute to legendary Mississippi blues artist Robert Johnson, who was just one among many others who made recordings there. Still, it would have been easy to go by and check it out. It may have been that when the

Playboys recorded there in 1935, they just got off the bus, took their equipment in, and played the songs Bob wanted to record, without any special awareness of the space where they made the recordings. When several members of our family and some Dallas friends, Jerry and Susi Grissom, got to tour the building in the 2010s, we walked around it as if we were being shown through the inner courts of heaven, but I expect Al didn't have a clue where it was. The difference in the two instances was that Al knew Cain's was still there when we were visiting Oklahoma in the 1960s. Why we didn't go see it made me wonder.

Al's job in downtown Dallas was at McCord's Music Company, where he was the manager of the piano and organ department. He was working there on November 22, 1963, the day President John F. Kennedy was assassinated. McCord's was one of the big retailers for musical instruments and sheet music and did a brisk business in music lessons. The McCord family was nice to Al, and it seemed to be a good place to work. I went with him to work every now and then and hung around the store. Most of the action seemed to be in the guitar section, where would-be rock 'n' rollers tried out guitars they couldn't afford to buy and traded licks with the sales staff, guys who were also would-be rock 'n' rollers in their spare time. Al would show people instruments, play a couple of songs for customers looking to put a piano or organ in their homes, and sometimes go to trade shows, showing off the offerings at McCord's. The store was on Elm Street, at the east end of downtown, not as far east as the famous Deep Ellum district, known for its connections with blues history, but pretty far east. The motorcade with President Kennedy, Jacqueline Kennedy, Texas Governor John Connally, and Nellie Connally went through downtown on Main Street, one block over from Elm. Al took his lunch break and walked over to watch the motorcade go by. There weren't a lot of people on the sidewalks at that particular part of the route, and Al hollered out, "Hey, Jack! Hey, Jackie!" He said they looked right at him and smiled as they went on their way to the other end of downtown, where Main, Elm, and Commerce Streets come together at the Triple Underpass. Al was walking back to McCord's and heard the gunshots coming from the other end of downtown. Like everyone else, he thought it was a car backfiring. Minutes later, Mr. McCord ran into the store saying the president had been shot. Al said everybody thought he was joking until they saw that he was crying.

Within minutes, everyone who worked downtown, and soon everyone around the world, heard the news of the shooting, shortly confirmed as the death of President Kennedy and the wounding of Governor Connally. Like countless people, we watched the television news coverage of the shootings, the arrest of Lee Harvey Oswald, and the shooting of Oswald while in police custody by Jack Ruby. Oswald was in the process of being transferred from Dallas Police headquarters to the Dallas County Jail when Ruby stepped out of the background and shot Oswald with a handgun. Ruby was a nightclub owner well known to police, and despite having a reputation for shady operations, he was able to freely move around the police station. Everything that weekend was televised, including Oswald's murder. Al and I were watching the broadcast and saw the shooting of Oswald, which added a degree of shock to an already shocking couple of days. When Al went back to work in Dallas on Monday, several of the sales staff were talking about Ruby. Because they played after-hours jobs, they knew many of the venues in Dallas, and they all knew Jack Ruby. He had bought musical instruments and gear from the store. Some of them had been to his club. It was all bizarre, on top of the deep sadness and shame that so many people in the Dallas area felt, that this terrible event had taken place in their city. Al never stopped thinking about the fact that he had been one of the last people to see John F. Kennedy alive.

In addition to the day jobs he had, Al continued to supplement the family finances with money he made playing pickup jobs at night with bands in the Fort Worth area, even making a few recordings with Bob from time to time. He had transferred his membership in the American Federation of Musicians to the Fort Worth local, and he kept in touch with what was going on and got jobs through the union and through his friendships with musicians in the area. In the same way that Bob was still in business in the 1960s, the reconstituted Light Crust Doughboys, having disbanded at the start of World War II, were active during this period. And Al knew Marvin "Smokey" Montgomery, Jerry Elliott, and other members of the Doughboys. By the late 1950s, Bob had stopped keeping a piano player in his band, but when he had a job in Fort Worth or Dallas, he would call Al and get him to sit in with the band, especially when they played at Panther Hall, the famous East Fort Worth dance hall. These jobs at Panther Hall were on Saturday night, and the then-independent Fort Worth television station, Channel 11, would broadcast a live half-hour from Panther Hall early in the evening before the actual dance began as part of its Saturday night country music programming, which included the Wilburn Brothers, Porter Waggoner, Cowboy Weaver, and other syndicated shows. It was a kick to see Al on TV with Bob Wills, and I'd watch, knowing they had broadcast live shows very much like these from Cain's Academy in Tulsa thirty years before.

The first time I met Bob Wills was at a recording session at Balch Springs near Dallas in 1965. I was happy to tag along and watch and listen to the action in the studio. It was a fascinating process for a first-time eyewitness to get to take in. They recorded five songs, two of which were released on the Longhorn label, a version of "Faded Love," Bob's classic hit from the 1940s, and an instrumental called "Wills Junction." And they are enjoyable songs to listen to. But I had been listening to the original recordings of the Playboys from the 1930s and '40s for years and had a good ear for what was happening in those tracks. I remember having the impression that this session in 1965 wouldn't live up to the excitement and creativity of those original recordings, maybe a glimpse of mortality for some of the legendary characters who had been part of our family's life for so long.

CHAPTER 8

Two Jobs

Betty's chronic health problems and the fact that she and Al never had anything even resembling a decent health insurance plan put constant stress on the family budget. It seemed that every time you turned around something new was wrong with her, on top of old problems that never seemed to go away. Betty didn't get Medicare coverage until 1986, so expenses for her care before that were the family's responsibility. She had numerous operations, countless visits to the family doctor and to various specialists, long stays in hospitals, and vast quantities of prescriptions. She knew a lot about drugs and drugstores, having worked in those places as a kid in Hominy and as an adult in Cleburne. In fact, her favorite boss of all time, Lamar Sloan, owned and ran the drugstore in Cleburne, where she had a lot of fun working as the bookkeeper. The two families were friends, and lots of good came of those relationships. For much of the 1960s, and off and on thereafter, she was well enough to work outside the home, at the drugstore and later keeping books at a factory in Cleburne and later still working for the City of Cleburne. She often seemed well enough to go to a full-time job, but then she'd come home sick and exhausted every night and need us to wait on her. What nobody knew then was that she had lupus. Some of her problems came from other sources, no doubt, but once the primary-care physician she started seeing in the 1980s figured out what was going on, a lot of things started to make sense. He got her off of a lot of the prescriptions she'd been taking. Then it was a matter of managing her symptoms, which the doctor and various nurses and aides helped her do. In that part of her life, she was able to get past some of the chronic pain and discomfort she had experienced for so long and do some volunteer work in the community, get together with friends to play Scrabble, and go to a weekly Bible study. But in the 1960s and '70s, it was rough.

Because of her frail health, Betty largely stopped being able to tend to the maintenance of the household. The common practice in those days was that the wife and mother would do all the "homemaking," but Nancy and Al took care of most of that work till Nancy got married, and she and Jerry set up their own household. In time, Al and Judy and I picked up most of those duties. Al took over most of the grocery shopping and cooking. Judy and I did most of the house-cleaning work. Al's vegetable production and canning efforts kept that part of the menu planning in good shape, but he also became quite an expert at tracking down bargains at the various mom-and-pop grocery stores around Cleburne. He would drive from one end of town to the other to save a dollar on something or other, which seemed to work against trying to save money. I always assumed he just liked going to all these places. The owners and workers were friendly. They were always glad to see him. It was a great slice of small-town life. There were only two or three banks in Cleburne then, and they kept big pads of checks on the counters in the local grocery stores. If you had an account with one of those banks and didn't have your checkbook, you'd just fill out one of the checks on the counter. Even as a kid, I wondered if anybody ever "paid for" something at one of those stores without the benefit of having an account at the bank whose check they were using. The stores also ran credit accounts and delivered groceries to people's homes. Our standby grocery was run by a man named Herman Smith.

Judy's and my house-cleaning system prompted a lot of jokes in the family, mostly at my expense. For instance, she organized a daily competition to see which of us could clean the most rooms. And because she could reach the kitchen sink and I couldn't, she always started there. She'd wash the dishes and do the other kitchen work while listening to the top-forty radio stations, while I sped through the rest of the house, hoping to win the house-cleaning race and the twenty-five-cent prize. I was so gullible that it took me an embarrassingly long time to realize she was hoodwinking me. I was proud of my long winning streak. For a good bit of this time, while Betty was able to work outside the home, she would be so wiped out when she got off that I used to wonder about the logic of it all. Of course, I never would have asked about it, but I finally figured it out. She worked because we needed the money. Doing housework was something the rest of us just did.

Life in this period was especially hard on Al, who worked just about nonstop to pay the costs of Betty's medical treatment. He nearly always had pickup jobs playing music at night in the post–Bob Wills years, but those were mostly the occasional Saturday night—and every New Year's Eve, of course—certainly not constant. Then, while he was working at McCord's Music in Dallas, he was approached by a guy in Fort Worth named Dave Winingham about playing the piano five or six nights a week at a new place Dave was about to open. It was called Napoleon's Pizza, and it was on the east side of Fort Worth. It was a great place. This was before the explosion of pizza restaurants in the U.S. There were three or four national chains that made decent pizza—not that anybody in North Texas was an expert on pizza then—but Dave Winingham had figured out how to make great pizza. And he built a raised stage in the restaurant, just big enough for a piano and a couple of chairs for additional musicians. Judy was in school at what was then called North Texas State University in Denton, and she and her buddies often drove down to Fort Worth to Napoleon's to eat some fantastic pizza and hear our dad play the piano and tell corny jokes. I suppose the "rinky-tink" piano craze of the '60s, associated with a national chain called Shakey's Pizza, was what got him the job. But he made it his own. For a while he played by himself. Then he had one or two other musicians join him, including Jerry Elliott, his old friend and longtime member of the Light Crust Doughboys, a fine musician and a truly nice guy. Others who played with him included a guitarist named Charlie Carpenter and banjo player Rayburn James. As Judy said, "He'd talk to the crowd and smile and bounce up and down on the piano bench and stomp his feet and act like a kid in a candy shop. Many people came almost every weekend to hear him, and so did I." When he'd take a break, he'd turn on a projector that showed silent movies, which, unlike the silent films at the old theater in Grandview, ran at Napoleon's without the benefit of a soundtrack. During those breaks, he'd visit with customers and make friends. Someone once showed him some home movies they'd taken of him and some of his mates playing. I asked him about it, and he deadpanned, "It looked like we were killing snakes."

One time he was headed from his job in Dallas to Fort Worth to get to Napoleon's and running a little late. But he really needed to go to the bathroom and stopped at a gas station somewhere between the two cities. This was before the whole Dallas-Fort Worth area grew together, and there were some fairly unsettled places along the way. It was also a time before just about every gas station became a convenience store. In those days, restrooms at gas stations tended to be outside and, often, around the corner from where the people working at the gas station might be. He pulled up to the door of the restroom, went inside, locked the door, did what he had come to do, and tried to open the door. But the doorknob came off in his hand. He tried to put it back in the door. That didn't work. He tried a couple of other things to get the door to open. None of that worked either. And he realized he was just locked in. He thought somebody would come along and need to go to the bathroom, turn the doorknob from the outside, and let him out. So he waited. And waited. After a long time, and this is after he was already running late and long before there were such things as cell phones, he realized it was awfully quiet around the gas station, and he got the strong impression that it had closed for the night. He began banging on the door and calling for help.

After a lot of that, a little kid came along and heard him. There's no telling what a kid was doing there, but Al figured he could help get him out of the mess he was in. The little kid heard the banging and said, "Hey, mister, what are you doing in there?" Al said, "I'm stuck in the bathroom. Try to open the door from the outside!" The kid responded, "Hey, mister, what are you doing in there?" Al didn't understand why he could hear what the kid was saying but the kid, who heard the banging on the door, couldn't hear what Al was saying. So he said the thing again about trying the door, and the kid asked again about what he was doing in there. So Al said, "Please go get a grownup. I need help getting out of here." They exchanged the same two sentences again, but the kid had one more speech in him. He changed it up a little bit this time and said, "Hey, mister. Why don't you come out of there?" Al thought, I'm stuck in this bathroom, and my only hope of getting out in the next fifteen hours is the dumbest kid in Texas. But sure enough, after another fifteen minutes or so, someone came along and opened the door and let him out. By then, he was in such a hurry to get to his job in Fort Worth that he didn't ask if his rescuer had been tipped off by the little kid. All someone needed to do to get him out of there was turn the outside doorknob, something that kid could have done right off the bat.

Napoleon's was fun for everybody, but it was hard on Al, even when he wasn't stuck in deserted filling stations. He worked in Dallas five days a week and played in Fort Worth six nights a week. He'd leave Cleburne around 7:30 a.m., nearly always stopping under a tree by the south side of Highway 67 between Alvarado and Midlothian to read the paper for a few minutes and break up the trip, get to work by nine, work all day, leave for Fort Worth by six, and be playing at Napoleon's by 7:30 p.m. He'd get off at about eleven and drive back to Cleburne, most nights by himself. One night he fell asleep after he crossed into Cleburne and ran into a signpost. Most of the times when I went to work with him in Dallas, I did that so I could be with him when he went to Napoleon's and when he drove home. I used to worry that he might crash the car or that something else bad was going to happen to him, especially after I found a handgun in the glove compartment of his car. I asked about it, and he reminded me that Napoleon's was in kind of a rough neighborhood in East Fort Worth and that a couple of times he'd been approached by groups of young men while he was stopped at red lights. When I didn't go with him, I would always try to stay awake until he got home. If he ever complained about this grueling schedule, I don't remember. He was mainly determined to pay Betty's medical bills. As always, they both had the view that you do whatever you have to do to take care of your debts. Napoleon's was great fun, but nobody could do much about the fact that it was part of an exhausting work and commuting schedule. It was mainly about paying the bills.

Al and Betty's attitude, of course, was shaped by what they had seen during the Great Depression. Betty, particularly, was struck by the sadness and shame she saw in the people who were on relief back then in her hometown of Hominy, Oklahoma. She was determined she'd never have to accept charity or walk away from a debt. About the maddest I ever saw her was one time when I came home from college for a weekend visit and had on a light blue work shirt. Those were popular then, and I'd gotten myself one. She met me at the door and said, "What the hell are you wearing?" She demanded to know where I'd gotten "that thing," and she couldn't believe it when I told her I'd actually paid money for it. "Well, don't wear it around in public," she said. "When I was a kid, that's exactly what Osage County gave people who were on relief!" She was proud that neither she nor her siblings back in Oklahoma ever had to wear government-issue clothing, and she was ashamed to think that I was wearing something very much like it on purpose. She thought everybody would think we were on welfare. I found something else to wear and never wore the shirt again around her.

This sensitivity of Betty's showed up in lots of ways, including one time when my Aunt Violet, the one who had mental limitations, was over at our house and wandered off for a while. Aunt Violet liked to come over and play the old piano her parents had bought for her when she was a kid. She could never keep it in her adulthood because she moved so often, usually after having exhausted the patience of a landlord. It would have been a nightmare to move that huge piano around with her. But on this occasion, Aunt Violet played and visited awhile and then went for a walk. She knew her way around our neighborhood, so her departure wasn't a cause for any particular alarm. After a half hour or so, however, the phone rang. It was Mrs. Whitehouse from the next house over, saying Violet was at her house and didn't we think she might want to come back to our house. The Whitehouse family lived on Forest Avenue. One side of our house faced across the alley from their backyard. So they weren't next-door neighbors, and our family never socialized with their family. They were always very nice to us, and their youngest daughter, Cheri, and I were the same age. We played together and got along well, except for one famous episode, when Cheri and another neighborhood girl, Marion James, got me down on the ground in Cheri's backyard while we were playing kickball so Marion could give me a black eye. I remember the black eye, but I don't remember what I said or did to deserve it. I'm sure it was justified. Marion and Cheri were not the kind to go around smacking people in the eye for no reason. Cheri's dad was a physician, though, and we were definitely not in their circle. Mrs. Whitehouse was hosting her bridge club or some such group, and Aunt Violet had no business being over there. Betty was mortified and said some unkind things about Violet and how embarrassing it was to have her wandering around the neighborhood, talking to the society ladies about being Alton's sister. I didn't know which embarrassed Betty more, the thought that Violet had imposed on a neighbor's party or the possibility that she'd said something outlandish while there.

Betty and I had occasional arguments about what I saw as her insensitivity, and I know she was displeased by my criticisms. Years later, long after she had died, I began to realize or admit what I didn't grasp back then, that her behavior might have been the result of the deep disappointment she felt. Life just hadn't worked out the way she had hoped it would. Then and later, I knew that to a certain extent she blamed Al for some of the rough times they'd been through, and I resented that on his behalf. But I became ashamed of how intolerant I was of her foibles. Sometimes they were minor. Sometimes they took the form of embarrassingly rude comments she would make to servers at restaurants and other people who displeased her. Anybody with her would have just tried to look invisible, which is what I tried to do. But I wish I'd had more tolerance for her bad behavior, shown her a little more grace. She was seldom unhappy alone; that is, if she was unhappy, she would make sure someone else was, too. But I should have tried harder to understand where that unhappiness was coming from. It seemed that Betty wanted to have a little fancier life than we had. Ours was one of the more modest houses in the neighborhood, and it was obvious that we were less affluent than a lot of folks who lived around in those blocks. They were always gracious and polite, but a little envy crept in, I think, and it ate at Betty.

Usually, Al's fun-loving nature compensated for a lot of Betty's sometimes cranky behavior. One of the ways that nature manifested itself was in his love of sound. He loved making music, but he also loved wordplay and giving people nicknames and using understatement. If something was great, he'd say it was "better than a sack of popcorn" or "better than a hack in the butt with a hatchet." Judy said, "He called my sister 'Butch' and my brother 'Sting-gone.' And I was 'Jude.'" She added that he called Nancy's kids, Leigh Anne, Jerry (who already had a nickname, "Pete"), and Robert, "Leigh Annie, Pedro, and Roberto." Some of Al's sounds were a little scary. Nancy's kids were staying with us one time. I was up late reading, and Pete heard remarkably loud snoring coming from Al's room and came to see me. He said, "David, there's a bear in Granddaddy's room!" I said, "Pete, that *is* Granddaddy!" Pete and Robert learned one of the family's most mysterious lessons, a strange way of tying shoes that Aunt Violet taught them that renders the laces essentially immune to coming untied.

Al wasn't a punster, but he got a kick out of language tricks, especially turning language in on itself. He liked that in speaking English, you could say something such as, "Turn in the book" or "turn the book in." But he would say, "Turn in the book in." It was a little thing, but he did it a lot, just because it was fun. He also loved inventing words. For instance, "boppa" for apple and "purtle" for turkey. He had weird expressions for other things. He called binoculars "well-wishers" and "eye-grabbers." I never figured out why. One I did ask him about was calling buses "separators," which he said he did because a bus could separate you from your life. He called Sand Flat, a little community between Cleburne and Grandview, "Lizard Lopes." He called little dogs "saucer asses" because they could sit on small plates, and he called eggs "hen fruit." One of our family's favorite expressions came from a time we were driving by the shore of the lake that supplied Cleburne's water and discussing the new sandy beach that had been installed and how much work it had taken to haul the sand in from somewhere, probably far away. Suddenly, Al said, "They hauled that sand in from somewhere, probably far away." From then on, anybody who said something someone else had just said was "hauling sand." Al would corrupt various sayings and lyrics of songs. For instance, he would sing the song "How Come You Do Me Like You Do," but instead of saying "how come," he would say "hook-em." Instead of "Franky and Johnny were sweethearts," he would sing, "Frankie and Johnny wore sweatshirts" and "Orange juice sorry you made me cry" instead of "aren't you?" Instead of saying "Rosetta," in the song of the same name, he said "raw setter, my raw setter," referring to one of his nicknames for a person's rear end. His favorite line when saying goodbye to someone was "Write if you find work." I did that a few times. He would always introduce the song "Under the Double Eagle" by saying, "Also known as 'Watch Out Below.'"

A lot of this came naturally. His family had odd sayings. For instance, anybody receiving medical care was "sick in bed with a doctor." An expectant mother was "looking for a baby." But Al was most famous among family and friends for Spoonerisms, trading the initial letters of words for other initials. Saying "larking pot" instead of parking lot or "dot-hog" instead of hotdog. There's no telling how many times a day he would say something like that, but on a good day it could be in the dozens. Sometimes his habit created accidental laughs when a Spoonerism of his ended up creating an off-color expression, but they usually came off without incident. An especially loved performance piece in the family was his Spoonerism version of "Loldigocks and the Bee Threars." He would go through the entire fairy tale, talking about how the soup was "hoo tot" or "rust jight" and how the bed was "hoo tard" or "soo toft." Kids were always astounded that he could keep turning words around like that for the whole time it took to tell the story.

One of the strangest word games Al played involved a code language that turned words inside out—that is, he would start the word with its regular initial letter and then add a Z sound and an F sound before finishing the end of the word. For instance, cat and dog became "cazzle-fat" and "dozzle-fog." Dad and Mom became "Dazzle-fad" and "Mozzle-fom." It didn't work on a word that started with F, for instance, fork. You could say "spoozle-foon" and "knizle-fife," but not "forzle-fork." That was illegal. Words with more than one syllable got to be intricate. *Reaction* became "reezle-fee azzle-faction." Doing this with a word as long as *responsibility* was considered dangerous and therefore discouraged. I've always regretted that I never asked him if he came up with this system of speech (speezle-feech), or if it originated in the long bus rides (buzzle-fus rizle-fides) around the Playboys' traveling circuit (cirzle-fircuit).

A similarly playful but remarkable feat he could accomplish musically was to play a fractured version of the novelty tune "Nola." It was one of those little songs with a tricky melody and a chord progression that was a bit challenging, at least for a novice. Al would play his way once through the song and then, on the second time through, begin to throw in a couple of wrong notes. You could always see a few people in the audience wince a bit when he did this. "Oh, the poor man. I think he's losing it." Then he would gradually move to where he was playing the melody in one key and the accompaniment in another key, letting everybody in on the joke. People who know a lot about playing the piano were always astounded to hear him do this. One very skilled pianist and organist told Al after hearing him play "Nola" that it was one of the most impressive things he'd ever seen a pianist do. Al was too polite to say, "I'm not a pianist. I'm a piano player." But the point was made. Only someone with a true mastery of the instrument and a highly developed sense of humor could have pulled that off. The famous Danish pianist and comedian Victor Borge did a similar version of "Nola" that might have given Al the idea, though I never thought to ask him that. Borge was a classically trained pianist, not someone who learned to play the way Al did. You might think it would have been easier for a formally trained pianist to play in two different keys at the same time, or it might make more sense that someone who didn't have to overcome as many rules, someone less formally trained, could do it more easily. Either way, it was always astonishing.

For a good bit of the 1960s, '70s, and early '80s, Al's day jobs were in Cleburne, mostly involving sales. If he ever wondered what he could have done for a career instead of selling things, I never heard him say it. But he did work a couple of times on the idea of publishing an instruction book for people who wanted to learn to play the piano by ear, the revival of his old "short method" from his days in Waco. He went to Nashville once and talked with some producers about possibly getting recording session work and visited a session with country singer Tommy Overstreet. The musicians knew Al was in the booth and when they finished the first song they were recording started playing "San Antonio Rose" in his honor. He appreciated that, and they were very nice to him, but there didn't seem to be much likelihood of breaking into the tight world of Nashville session players. In fact, there just weren't any serious possibilities for him that didn't involve sales of furniture, pianos, and organs, and, later, advertising, for the radio station and then for the newspaper in Cleburne. He worked for a while at KCLE, the local radio station that had aired his remote broadcast of "Bargains with Music," from back when he worked for Dickson's furniture store. As a staff member at KCLE, he had a combination of duties including selling advertising and producing some programs for broadcast. This seemed to me the coolest job he'd had since leaving the band, and I think he enjoyed doing the shows. In a way, he was going back to the early days of his career as a musician. He would play live on the air from time to time, and he recorded commercials for local businesses and did interviews with people around town for human-interest stories. He talked about growing up in Johnson County and old-timers he remembered and had a good time doing all of this work. One of his great friends was the Cleburne High School head football coach, Bob Wright. Somehow Al discovered that Coach Wright was a great music lover and a fine singer, and the two of them began appearing around town and entertaining at meetings of civic clubs and the like. Coach Wright came over to our house often and sang popular songs to Al's accompaniment with words supplied by Betty, who had a great memory for lyrics. And during this time, Al would interview Coach Wright for KCLE every week during football season. They made a good radio pair. Along with talking about the team's performance that week and prospects for the game coming up, they would talk about music, old friends, and their experiences growing up in small Texas towns. Coach Wright had a great sense of humor and a funny, homespun manner in his storytelling. Al would ask him what was going on with the team, and the coach would describe the players and the upcoming games with a folksy style that Al really got a kick out of. Folksy was something Al did well. His commercials and promotional spots for local businesses and civic concerns would be considered amateurish and corny now, but he delivered them with the combination of humor and seriousness that people who really care about what they're describing can achieve.

When he was having a conversation with someone on the radio, such as Bob Wright, Al's voice sounded much like his normal voice. He used his more "professional" voice when he did commercials. He was the same way when being interviewed. He was on Bill Mack's "Open Road" overnight show on WBAP in Fort Worth several times, and I was always struck by how different he sounded. It was the same when he spoke into a microphone at a performance. It wasn't that he sounded more formal. It was more like he was trying to separate his performing self from his regular self. To say he was "putting on an act" sounds like he was being artificial, untrue to himself. That wasn't it. I think that part of it went back to that early schooling in public speaking. His voice just sounded bigger, more like somebody who was letting the audience hear part of him that wasn't ordinarily available. It fascinated me and made me a little uncomfortable sometimes, but it made me glad I was getting in on this secret personality, all at the same time.

As he did to my sisters, Al seemed to a lot of my friends like a big kid. I didn't necessarily see that, but I always had sense enough to appreciate his humor and dedication to making people happy. He was also an avid reader, especially interested in history, and he loved the Classics Illustrated series. He read those to me when I was a kid. *Les Miserables*, *The Red Badge of Courage*, *Lorna Doone*, and *A Tale of Two Cities* were our favorites. I didn't realize until I was well into grade school that those were based on "real" books that grownups read. At the same time, he didn't care a bit that someone might think it was weird that he read comic books. It was something he enjoyed, and he passed that enjoyment along to me. In fact, as first grade approached and I didn't seem very excited about starting school, he told me that if I got motivated and went to school, I'd be able to read comic books on my own. I hadn't gone to kindergarten and wasn't much of a reader at the age of six. He always got a kick out of telling how I came home from the first day of first grade, picked up a comic book, and was disappointed to find out his prediction hadn't come true. I couldn't read a comic book any more effectively that afternoon than I could have before I left for school that morning.

Among the fathers in our neighborhood crowded with kids, he was one of the easiest to be around and certainly one of the funniest. Two of the other dads who were a lot of fun were Ed

Gray, the father of my best friend in the neighborhood, Steve Gray, and the owner of a menswear store in downtown Cleburne, and John A. James, a state district judge and the father of one of the neighborhood girls my age, Marion, the one who gave me the black eye. Both these men were hilarious. Ed had a super-dry sense of humor and lots of funny nicknames for people and organizations. He called the local Cleburne newspaper "The Blister." The James family had a dog named Doug who was an escape artist. Marion would say, "Doug dug out of his dugout, and now we are Dougless." When they rounded him up again, Judge James would say, "I bring you greetings from Douglas Dog, who is back in custody." But Al was right up there with the funny dads. He cracked up my college friends Rick Long and Allen Atkinson one time by telling why he preferred fried okra to boiled: "That slimy stuff. I was always afraid if I ate some of it, when I got up from dinner, it would be sitting in my chair." Pretty disgusting, but funny to my friends. Other college friends also loved being around both Betty and Al. A lot of them knew about Betty's secret nickname "Sweet Thing" and took to calling Al "Big Al." Friends Mike and Teresa Gibson earned fame when Teresa got mixed up one time and referred to them as "Sweet Al and Big Thing." Betty didn't know about "Sweet Thing" until late in life, when someone let it slip in her presence.

Sometimes it's hard to imagine musicians and other creative people having interests in normal activities. But Al was very interested in sports, gardening, the care of pecan trees, and so on. He always loved fishing and had a number of friends who owned lakes or ponds stocked with fish. He never tried fly fishing or deep-sea fishing, as far as I know. His favorite thing was to sit on a pier or in a boat and just cast out into the water, especially looking for smaller fish: perch, crappie, and bream. He always complained if stormy weather interfered with his fishing and once said he wanted his headstone to read, "Here lies a man who hated wind." He would go dove hunting every now and then if someone invited him. And he hunted squirrels on the farm, but mainly as a method of protecting the pecan trees from the pests on the old home place. Judy has stories about going squirrel hunting with Al when she was a kid and wondering why he kept looking up in the trees when she thought they ought to be looking for squirrels on the ground. He was quite skilled at pruning, budding, and grafting trees and kept a supply of cheese cloth and paraffin on hand. It was striking how much that work resembled bandaging cuts on a person's arms or legs, and the care he took with it seemed to make sense of the use of the word *nursery* to describe working with plants, along with the expression *tree surgery*. His farm background and love of eating fresh vegetables kept him constantly at work on a garden. He tried to start a garden in the backyard of the house in Cleburne, but the soil there was poor. He did better with a couple of larger plots he kept around town. His specialty was corn, but he also grew okra, beans, and peas, and he loved cooking all those things as well as growing them. He showed his farm upbringing often, for instance, by making a meal out of what he called "crumble in," a large bowl filled with a skillet's worth of cornbread covered with a quart of buttermilk. I thought it was revolting, but he loved it.

Al's love of sports took a lot of forms. He played golf from time to time, also a little tennis. But he really loved spectator sports. He watched a lot of baseball on television, especially the "game of the week" in those days before sports programming became the around-the-clock force of nature it is now. Like most people in the Dallas-Fort Worth area, we became instant Dallas Cowboy fans as soon as that NFL franchise started up in 1960. There was an unfortunate rule that wouldn't allow local broadcast of an NFL game if the game hadn't sold out. The Cowboys played in the old Cotton Bowl stadium then, in Dallas's Fair Park, and it took them several years to become competitive, so there were quite a few games with tickets left over. Channel 4, the CBS affiliate in Dallas, would show those games if they sold out, and we picked up the Dallas and Fort Worth stations using the antenna on the roof of the house in Cleburne, which was pointed north toward those cities. If the game didn't sell out, Channel 4 would show some NFL game we didn't care about in another city, so someone would have to get on the roof of our house and turn the antenna south, toward Waco, so we could try to get the broadcast from down there. Waco is just enough farther from Cleburne than Dallas that this was a fairly big production, with often spotty results. But we were a Cowboys family, so that was that. We went to see the Cowboys play in the Cotton Bowl a few times. At one of those games, we were sitting next to one of the end zones, and the Cowboys weren't doing particularly well. The Cowboy quarterback, Don Meredith, who deserved a lot of credit for getting the Cowboys to the point of being taken seriously in the NFL, was often criticized for his partying lifestyle. His critics gave him the nickname "Dandy Don." In the game we were watching, he had thrown a couple of interceptions, and the crowd was getting a little cranky. The Cowboys were backed up to the goal line, close to where we were sitting, and there weren't a lot of people in that part of the stadium, so you could hear some of what the players were saying to each other—and there was a good chance they could hear some of what people in the stands were yelling. Just as Meredith came up to the line of scrimmage to start the next play, a man sitting in front of us hollered out, "Which team you gonna throw to this time, *Dandy Don*?" We thought that was a tacky thing to say, but it was kind of funny.

Al loved going to Southwest Conference football games and loved just about as much going to the Cleburne High games. When Judy became the head coach of the girls' basketball team at Arlington High School, Al became a rabid fan of her team. He traveled to dozens of games over the years in Arlington and all over Texas and became a beloved figure for Judy's players. He also loved track and field, partly because of his track experiences in his student days. We went to the Southwest Conference Outdoor Track and Field Championships for several years and went to indoor meets at Will Rogers Coliseum in Fort Worth, where we also saw the magnificent Harlem Globetrotters. And when the Washington Senators moved to Arlington and became the Texas Rangers, he enjoyed going to their games. I ran track throughout junior high and high school, and Al loved to go to our meets. He even came to our workouts. At this point, in the late 1960s and spring 1970, while he was working at the newspaper in Cleburne, he had a flexible schedule and often showed up at our track workouts. One member of our team took to calling him Coach Stricklin. We still ran distances in yards then, not meters, and I always amazed my teammates when I told them that he had run the hundred-yard dash in 9.9 seconds in the 1920s.

His old disappointment about not having had a real chance to run well at the regional track meet in high school, and similar experiences, gave Al a lifelong bias in favor of underdogs. This showed up especially in his feelings about sports teams. Despite his mixed experience at Baylor, he always loved the university and rooted for Baylor sports teams, even when those teams weren't doing so well, which, in those days, was often. Based on this preference for underdogs, his fanatical support of Judy's basketball teams was harder to understand than his loyalty to my track team. The track teams I was on never came close to winning a meet, while Judy never had a losing season in her whole career. That proves his dad loyalty, with respect to Judy's teams, was stronger than his underdog bias. Al was also proud of a distant cousin, Bailey Howell, who played for the Boston Celtics in their glory years and who had overcome his segregated Tennessee and Mississippi background to become the great Bill Russell's road-trip roommate and good friend. But Al's truest passions for certain teams were equaled by his hatred of others, especially the perennially successful. He hated the New York Yankees, for instance. He didn't really care that much for any other Major League baseball teams, but he was automatically for anybody who was playing the Yankees. He would often say, "I wouldn't root for the Yankees if they were playing Russia!" The same went for Notre Dame's great football teams, those of the University of Texas under Darrell Royal, and those of the University of Alabama when Bear Bryant was coaching. Al often called Bryant "Water Walker" because of the reverence Alabama fans had for him, and he made a point of saying this nickname with a very distinct, fake Deep South accent. Years later, when Al got to know Darrell Royal when the Texas Playboys started getting invited to the celebrity golf tournaments that Royal and Willie Nelson hosted to raise money for charity, Al had to admit that Royal was a nice guy, but he still cherished the memory of hating those old Longhorn teams. His passion for the underdog was something deep in Al and something he instilled in his kids.

Betty wasn't much interested in spectator sports, but she kept two sports-celebrity crushes going, one for golfer Arnold Palmer and one for University of Oklahoma head football coach Bud Wilkinson. She would watch golf tournaments and OU football games on television so she could call out, "There's my boyfriend!" when Palmer or Wilkinson came on screen. Two of her old friends from Oklahoma,

Floyd and Esther Jackson, lived for a number of years in Corpus Christi, Texas, which meant they lived farther from us in Cleburne than if they had stayed in Oklahoma. But they were big OU football fans and liked to go to the annual slugfest at the Cotton Bowl between OU and Texas. Everybody around where we were called it the "OU game" and had enthusiasm for the Texas Longhorns because they nearly always had some former Cleburne boys playing for them and because, of course, we were actually living in Texas. But Betty pulled for the Sooners because of her origins and because of her crush on their coach. The game always took place during the Texas State Fair, whose grounds contained the Cotton Bowl. The weekend always featured lots of drunkenness in downtown Dallas, arrests of fans of both teams, and a spirited match once the game got underway. Betty and Al went to the game a few times with Floyd and Esther. Floyd was not a big guy, but for some reason everybody called him "Solid." (I always thought "Solid Jackson" would be a great name for a character in a detective novel.) On one of those Texas-OU weekends the four of them got on an elevator in their hotel and found themselves surrounded mostly by OU fans. Betty and the Jacksons were wearing OU buttons, but a very large, very drunk OU fan insisted on asking everyone on the elevator where they were from and berating anybody from Texas. When he got to Floyd and asked him where he was from, he said, "Corpus Christi . . . Oklahoma." The big guy said, "Fine town. Been there many times." Luckily, the elevator got to their floor before Betty and Al had to say they were from Cleburne, Oklahoma.

Betty's strong opinions and blunt way of expressing herself were legendary around Cleburne and among our friends and family. It's putting it mildly to say she was quick with a sassy comment, such as the time she and Al were driving through the courthouse square in Cleburne, and our only despised relative, by marriage, stepped out in front of them, jaywalking. As Al slammed on the breaks to keep from hitting him, Betty said, "Well, you'll never have another chance like that." Another strong opinion she expressed when I was young was that one piano player in the family was plenty. I had expressed some interest in learning to play, and I pecked around on the piano in our living room every now and then. Aunt Violet showed me some chords and a little bit about rhythm. She also showed me the first guitar chords I ever learned. But Al and I didn't sit down and play much because of a warning Betty gave me. I was about ten years old, and somebody asked me if I planned to be a piano player like my dad. Before I could answer, Betty said, in a voice that sounded at least half serious, "If he ever tries that, I'll slam the lid on his hands and break all his fingers!" She was not an abusive mother. I knew she was kidding, but it did have some effect on my ideas of playing in her presence. Her feelings about being married to a musician were complicated. She wasn't crazy about the fact that many Saturday nights her husband was off playing a job somewhere, or that every New Year's Eve for years and years found her at home by herself. Before I was old enough to go to New Year's Eve parties on my own, she and I would stay up till midnight, watch Guy Lombardo and His Royal Canadians, and have some 7 Up in champagne glasses. She wouldn't have slammed the piano lid on my fingers, but I think she did feel that one piano player in the family was enough. Part of her attitude arose from an age-old dilemma for spouses of musicians, especially musicians in dance bands. She loved to dance but hated to go to dances where Al was playing. She said band wives were "as useless as tits on a boar hog." It was boring, lonely, and annoying to see the attention her husband got while she sat there with other women she might not like or even know.

Unattached men at dances seemed to know that a table with seven or eight women sitting by themselves was made up of "the wives" and left them alone. If she'd been asked, I don't know if she would have danced with a man she didn't know. And I think another part of her resistance to my learning to play the piano came from her feeling that a musician's life was too uncertain and certainly not lucrative enough.

Betty had a lot of rules, and she marked people down if they broke one of them, but she also had a lot of funny sayings. Some of her rules were the standard ones. Men were supposed to hold doors open for ladies. Opening the door for anybody seemed like a good practice, so I didn't have a problem with it. But it seemed important to her because it reinforced traditional gender roles. Men should hold chairs for women while they were easing into them. Somewhat unnecessary, but okay. She also said, "Don't sit in the car honking the horn like an idiot when you go to someone's house to pick them up. Get out and go knock on the door as if you might have some sense." Also, no problem. That's just rude. Some of her other rules were kind of strange. Several had to do with beds. You couldn't sit on a bed in street clothes or store anything under a bed. And you couldn't put a hat on a bed. That one, she said, was to ward off bad luck, one of the few superstitions I was aware she had. And you couldn't leave a closet or cabinet door open longer than the time it took to put something in or get something out. Some of her funny expressions were meant to sound ferocious to make you stop doing something she didn't like, such as, "If you don't straighten up, I'll knock fire from your skull." I was always a little fascinated by that one, imagining what that would look like. She also had her own set of funny sayings, not to be outdone by her creative husband. She often prefaced them with, "As my mother used to say," and then,

"You're as handy as a pocket on a shirt," "He's as stubborn as a government mule," or "She's as independent as a hog on ice." She usually added "whatever that means" to that last one. If she was worn out, she'd say, "I'm so tired I'm crazy," or "I'd stretch a mile if I didn't have to walk back." Someone small wasn't even "as big as a minute." If you butted in on her business, she'd say, "Tend to your own knitting." If you sassed her during a meal, she would point a fork at you and say, "Hang your eye on that." I don't remember any whippings she gave me, but she once told me she whipped me five times in the same day when I was a little kid for going out into the street in front of our house. She used that as an example of someone who was as stubborn as a government mule. I used to say that I was ten before I found out my middle name wasn't "Dammit."

She was smart, blunt, opinionated, and convinced she was right about everything that mattered to her. And she enjoyed a good argument. We talked a lot, about the issues of the day, news coverage of what was going on, crazy stuff happening in our family and with our friends, often arguing—mostly good-naturedly—about various things. She and I had a spectacular argument about Willie Nelson one night at home in Cleburne. I was making the case that Nelson was a brilliant songwriter and interpreter of a wide range of people's experiences, and I was specifically pointing out his work on pathbreaking albums such as *Phases and Stages*. I said that he may not have created the concept album, but he had taken it to a great height. I thought I had her with the point that one side of the album is about a man's perspective on a doomed relationship, and the other is about a woman's. Despite her preference for old-fashioned gender roles, she was pretty receptive to what was then called women's liberation, partly because she had experienced discrimination at work, often finding herself doing her bookkeeping job and a good bit of the job of her male boss, who was making a lot more money than she was and taking credit for her work. I became sympathetic to efforts in favor of women's equality from an early age because of the ways she was taken advantage of by male coworkers and supervisors. Pointing out that Willie presents a woman's viewpoint on one side of the album seemed like a potential advantage in our argument. But in any event, I said, you just have to recognize that this is someone with a lot of talent. We'd been going for probably a half hour when she stood up suddenly and walked out of the room. I couldn't believe it. She had never just gotten up and abandoned a full-on argument. I sat there stunned for about a minute. Then she walked back in with a dictionary in her hand, and called out, "*Talent*. A noun: creative or artistic aptitude." And off the argument went again. It was so funny, and one of my favorite experiences with her. That was a time Betty's sassy personality was fun.

Sometimes it wasn't fun. A lot of the time, anything that popped into her head would come right out of her mouth. Sometimes that was funny. But she could make cutting remarks that made people feel small, sometimes outright insulted. And she got very judgmental as she got older, especially during the '60s and '70s when kids stopped dressing and grooming the way she thought they should. Because I figured out most of her rules pretty early, I mostly stayed out of the doghouse with her. But I thought that she associated rules of etiquette with being middle-class and that abiding by them would make her feel we were in fact members of the middle class, a status that sometimes felt we were hanging onto by our fingernails, especially by comparison to some of our neighbors. She and Al seldom argued loudly, never violently. But there was often disapproval, and certainly disappointment, coming from Betty. And it could be aimed in lots of directions, not just toward him. She dealt with some of those feelings by constantly trying to upgrade the house. It was a modest, three-bedroom frame house with a bathroom and a half. When I was a kid we had an attic fan, which I thought was fantastic. Also, an evaporator cooler in Judy's bedroom that blew like a cyclone. She and I would hook a sheet onto that cooler and inflate it like a tent while we cranked up the radio and listened to KNOK and KFJZ out of Fort Worth, KLIF-Dallas, WLS-Chicago, and Wolfman Jack on XERF, coming from Cuidad Acuña, across the Rio Grande from Del Rio. Then Betty decided these methods of cooling the house were unfashionable, and, once she scrounged up the money, we got central air conditioning. Same with the great hardwood floors in that house. One day some guys showed up to put down wall-to-wall carpeting. That was what everybody was getting, so that's what we got. Eventually, as Al's income increased, Betty started wearing diamond rings and even got a stole made of some kind of fur. I always tried to walk a few feet away from her when she wore it. Not because of fear of being accosted by animal-rights protestors. That wasn't much of a thing where we were then. I just thought it was tacky and that she was putting on airs.

Al had a different combination of feelings, something a lot of people misunderstood about him. He always seemed so relaxed and cheerful around other people, and he was a delight to be around most of the time, but most people never knew about the struggles in the back of his mind. This was one of the ways he was a true performer, always "on," always aware of the effect he might be having on his audience. The cheerful, sometimes hammy entertainer had come of age when jazz was still in its infancy. After all, the first money he ever made playing music was for accompanying a silent film! He didn't care if he seemed corny or old-fashioned. He was determined to make people glad they'd come to see him play the piano, and that attitude colored the way he behaved when he was around just about anybody, especially people from outside the family. He hated pretense and snobbery, but I don't think I ever saw him behave rudely toward anyone who was putting on airs or thought they were better than other people. Even his fondness for underdogs didn't prompt him to berate anybody who was successful, keeping in mind that he never met Bear Bryant, and I bet that he would have liked the famous coach if he had ever met him. Al had occasion to meet a lot of famous people in his time, especially musicians, and I never had the least impression that he begrudged anyone their success. I think that his training with Bob Wills really stayed with him. It went beyond the old idea that the customer is always right. It had to do as well with an idea that when people come to see you, they ought to leave happy.

My sisters and I have sometimes wondered if he had a happy life. There certainly were times when it seemed that he was supremely happy, especially when he was performing. But you always had to wonder if his apparent happiness was itself a performance, if he was only pretending to be happy. It was another way he worked two jobs. One of his jobs was taking care of the family financially. The other was trying to look okay while under the pressure of everything. The day jobs he had after leaving the Texas Playboys didn't seem to be much fun, and sometimes they were just downright awful. Playing music regularly, especially on weekends and some holidays, always a job on New Year's Eve, was more than a hobby for him and more than a part-time job that brought in some extra money. It was a big part of who he was. But most of what he did for his main work was selling things. His job at the *Cleburne Times-Review* occasionally prompted him to write an article, usually about his exploits in the music world and about old stories of Johnson

County, Cleburne, and Grandview. But mostly the newspaper job involved selling advertising. One of the few times he really shocked me was when he told me once when I was in high school that he hated selling. I said, "But you're so good at it. Everybody says that." "Yeah," he answered. "Everybody says that because I make them think I'm good at it, but I don't like it." He told me that almost every day job he'd had since leaving the Texas Playboys had been something he hadn't enjoyed doing. The greatest time in his life was when he was playing with Bob and the band in the 1930s and '40s, and I think he knew that he was luckier than most people. How many people get to do something so truly remarkable, with a wonderfully creative boss and a path-breaking organization? But remembering those days and how great they had been didn't make the loss of those experiences sting any less. The pickup music jobs he got playing around the Fort Worth area were something. They were often enjoyable, sometimes very enjoyable. But they certainly weren't the Texas Playboys.

CHAPTER 9
Reunited

And then they were back. Al's long absence from Bob and the band wasn't something the family talked much about, and nobody I knew younger than Al and Betty even knew much about it, if anything. But then it cranked up again. Al was still working for the newspaper in Cleburne when his career as a musician reignited, and his family was about as surprised as anyone that it happened. The band's reunification marked the move into the last phase of his life and became the second of the happiest times of that life, the first, of course, being his time with a young family in Tulsa, playing with Bob and the band in the 1930s and '40s. With the rediscovery of the Texas Playboys in the 1970s, that last, happy moment arrived for Brother Al.

It didn't happen all at once. Bob's health problems, coupled with the generosity he had shown so many people over so many years, had left him in precarious financial shape. There were some benefit performances organized by promoters and other music-business friends Bob had, which got old Texas Playboys together, along with lots of country performers and other celebrities. There were the famous recording sessions in 1973 that resulted in *For the Last Time*, when Al, Leon McAuliffe, Leon Rausch, Smoky Dacus, Eldon Shamblin,

Johnny Gimble, and Keith Coleman played with Bob in the studio the first day of the two-day session in Dallas. Merle Haggard arrived for the second day, though not in time to record with Bob, as he had dreamed of doing for most of his life, because of a stroke Bob had in the night after the first day of recording. There were one-off performances such as the 1974 appearance Al made at the Ritz Theater in Austin with Asleep at the Wheel. Just about every living former Texas Playboy gathered in Tulsa for Bob's funeral on May 15, 1975, and quite a few of them played some music for the occasion. But nothing seemed to point toward reuniting the band until later in 1975, when some of the guys from the original band started having conversations with Bob's widow, Betty Anderson Wills, about the fact that there might be an audience for a reconstituted version of the Texas Playboys. There wasn't any telling whether people would respond to the Texas Playboys without Bob Wills. But what with the fans from the old days who were still around and the sizable number of young people who—because of Asleep at the Wheel and other new bands—were showing an interest in Bob, his music, and his story, it seemed worth trying. Leon McAuliffe was the natural choice for bandleader. He had fronted his own band for years after his time with Bob, and, of course, he was the legendary steel guitarist who had helped make the band so popular in the 1930s. There were still several fiddlers around from the old days, plus some of the great guitarists, and the original rhythm section, including Smoky Dacus and Al. A deal was worked out to share the band's income with Betty Wills, and Bob Wills's Original Texas Playboys began to take shape.

Bob and Betty Wills and Al and Betty Stricklin had spent quite a bit of time together in the early 1970s. Bob had his first stroke in 1969, and Al and Betty Stricklin enjoyed helping Bob and Betty Wills make driving trips to Nashville and such places. And Al often made the thirty-mile drive from Cleburne to see Bob in Fort Worth, where he and Betty lived for the last years of Bob's life. On some of those visits, because of the damage from his stroke, Bob struggled to talk. One time, they were listening to recordings of the band, and "Roly Poly" came on, the tune whose lyrics puzzled me when I was a little kid. The song opens with a piano solo by Millard Kelso, who had followed Al as Bob's piano player. Kelso was a fine musician, but he tended to get a little ahead of, or "rush," the beat, which drove Bob crazy. When Kelso's solo came up, Al told me Bob scrunched up his face and held up his hand with his thumb and index finger apart a little bit. Al said, "Kelso rushing?" Bob just nodded his head. They became good friends, beyond their former boss-employee relationship, and the two Bettys became very close as well. Al and Betty had married after Al was no longer with Bob Wills, and so she had missed the experience of being the wife of a Texas Playboy during their heyday in Tulsa. The ups and downs of Al and Betty's life as a married couple were sometimes marked by Betty's mixed feelings about Al's fame, modest though it was for most of their married life. This time, she found herself enjoying the fame and what came with it, I'd say more often than not, especially an event that took place in Cleburne.

That experience was the visit of Bob Wills and Merle Haggard to Al and Betty's house. Haggard had been working on getting more of a Bob Wills sound for portions of the stage show he put on with his band, the Strangers. Haggard had loved Bob's music from his early days growing up in the Bakersfield, California, area. He also loved the classics of country music, did passable imitations of some of the great country vocalists, and recorded a tribute album to Jimmie Rodgers, the "Father of Country Music." It was only natural that Haggard would record a Bob Wills album, which turned out to be *A Tribute to the Best Damn Fiddle Player in the World*. He gathered several guys who had played with Bob—including Eldon Shamblin, Johnny Gimble, Joe Holley, and Bob's brother Johnnie Lee—and made the album in 1970. He got George French to play piano, thinking Al must have died because Millard Kelso and some other post-Al Playboy piano players were gone. So Al wasn't invited to be part of the session for the tribute album. Haggard was wrong, of course, and when he learned that Al was still around, he made a point of getting to know him. Al and Betty made a trip in 1971 to Haggard's house in Bakersfield, staying with him for a few days. Al played Haggard's white grand piano, and the two of them discussed the idea that Al might write a book about his years with Bob Wills and His Texas Playboys, which, in fact, he did. Once Al got into the writing, Haggard asked him to tape-record himself reading the manuscript. Al got a reel-to-reel machine, made the tapes, and sent them to Haggard. Haggard's encouragement of the surviving Playboys to get together and play music with each other helped plant the seed of the idea several years later to reconstitute the band. I'm sure there were other former Playboys who helped give Haggard the idea of having these Playboy reunions, but we always thought his conversations with Al were important in that whole process.

Haggard played a benefit show for Bob at the Tarrant County Convention Center in Fort Worth in March 1972 with Tex Ritter, Roy Acuff, Little Jimmy Dickens, and lots of other country performers and various celebrities. And he invited Al and Betty and several others to have dinner with him at the performance venue. I took my lifelong friend Landa Sloan, the daughter of Betty's former boss at the drug store in Cleburne, to meet everybody. Haggard was very nice to Landa, though he couldn't get her first name straight during the introductions to his band and crew. She quickly became known as "Al and Betty's little friend Linda" after Al, who had known Landa all her life, got so excited about introducing her to Haggard that he said her name wrong. Landa always got a kick out of that. This Fort Worth get-together prompted the visit to Cleburne. Haggard and several of the band and crew members cooked up a plan to meet at the Stricklin house later that year and have a jam session and possibly make some recordings. The gathering took place right after Christmas, and we had to take down the Christmas tree and move some furniture out of the living room because of the expected crowd. And it was a crowd. Haggard was still married then to Bonnie Owens, a very nice person. She was there, and so were the great former Playboy fiddler Johnny Gimble and his gifted musician son, Dick Gimble, who brought his bass guitar. The legendary Sleepy Johnson was there. Sleepy was in Bob's band in Fort Worth well before the Texas Playboys came into existence and was quite accomplished on guitar, banjo, and fiddle. Two of the great old-time fiddlers from Fort Worth, brothers Norman and Vernon Solomon, were there. Al played the piano that sat in the living room, the one he had learned to play on. Haggard sang and played the fiddle, which he was eager to show Bob he had been working to master. Haggard had created a bit of excitement when he pulled into Cleburne in his tour bus and stopped on South Main Street at Ed Ball's Grocery. He went in himself to ask if anybody knew how to get to Al Stricklin's house. Mr. Ball later reported that he recognized Haggard and was happy to provide the famous musician the directions to Al's home. Word got around town that something was going on at Al and Betty's, and we were told that quite a few people drove by the house on West Fifth Street to see Haggard's bus. A couple of Haggard's crew members set up some recording equipment. A microphone was hung from a light fixture, and the music began. Bob was in his wheelchair. Betty Wills, his devoted, wonderful wife, checked on him throughout the evening. Betty Wills, Betty

Stricklin, and Bonnie Owens had a fun visit. Great stories and music went around the room that night.

Even more important to the former Texas Playboys than Merle Haggard's interest in them was the invitation to appear on the first broadcast of the first season of *Austin City Limits*. The producers of the new show had done a pilot with Willie Nelson in 1974, and the first season of regular programs was to begin in 1976 with Asleep at the Wheel, who helped arrange for guys from the Original Texas Playboys to be on the show with them. The show was taped in September 1975, just a few months after Bob's death, in a studio of the public television station on the campus of the University of Texas. It was a remarkable event. The band on that occasion consisted of Al on piano, Leon McAuliffe on steel guitar and vocals, Leon Rausch on bass and vocals, Tommy Alsup and Bob Kizer on guitars, Smoky Dacus on drums, and Jesse Ashlock, Sleepy Johnson, and Keith Coleman on fiddles. The guys showed up for the sound check, and members of Asleep at the Wheel were astonished that they didn't see the need for much of a rehearsal. Some of the Playboys hadn't played together in over thirty years. Some hadn't ever played together! But they knew that anybody who had ever played with Bob Wills could play with everybody *else* who had ever played with Bob Wills. The Wheel played first and recorded plenty of numbers for the eventual *Austin City Limits* broadcast. My impression was that the producers thought the Playboys would play a couple of songs and that would be it. But the live audience went so crazy that the Playboys had to keep going. They did several of their most famous songs, with heavy emphasis on fiddles, and a medley of fiddle tunes in tribute to Bob by Jesse, Sleepy, and Keith, who also did his uncanny Bob Wills impression, which was a crowd pleaser. It was a great experience, and the guys had a wonderful time. There were many mentions of Bob and his legacy, and it was obvious that there was an appetite for Bob's music and that the Original Texas Playboys should help satisfy that appetite.

The next night, the guys played a dance at the Broken Spoke, the legendary South Austin honky-tonk. And that really was something. The handful of benefits and other shows various Playboys had done in the previous few years were all at concert venues. But the Broken Spoke was a dance hall, the natural habitat of western swing, Bob Wills, and the Texas Playboys. The rhythm, in two senses of the word, of a Bob Wills dance was there. Not just the rhythm of the dance numbers, but also the rhythm of how the Playboys moved from number to number, their interactions with the dancers, the talking among the band members as they worked with Leon McAuliffe in on-the-spot arrangements—it was so completely natural that everyone there that night seemed to know they were experiencing something very special. And the Playboys really were like kids who had been given the keys to the toy shop. Everybody associated with the band was excited by the overwhelming reception they had gotten from the young people, especially, at the *Austin City Limits* taping and at the Broken Spoke and knew it meant something, maybe a lot. Smoky was the most visibly moved by it. He told me, "There was real love going on in that place."

After they got off, back at the Villa Capri, the venerable Austin motor hotel just off of the University of Texas campus where the *Austin City Limits* folks had put them up, they staged what came to be called the Mark Spitz Water Follies. Spitz was a wondrously successful American Olympic swimmer in those days, and when the guys got back from playing, several of them just jumped into the Villa Capri swimming pool, making a terrific racket at an hour that was surely after the official closing time for the pool. It just called for some sort of celebration, an expression of jubilation. Al's granddaughter Sarah met Asleep at the Wheel leader Ray Benson years later at Kerrville, and the story of the swimming pool at the Villa Capri was the one he wanted to make sure Sarah knew. Ray's version was that Al stripped down to his jockey shorts. I don't remember what anybody had on, but I remember Al, Leon Rausch, and Tommy Alsup in the pool. Though this was all happening pretty late, word around the place was that the Texas Playboys were staying there, and anybody who was disturbed by the ruckus probably figured it was for a good cause. The band was indeed back.

The *Austin City Limits* appearance, the Broken Spoke job, and a few other performances were attended mostly by new converts to the Wills/Texas Playboys story, pulled in by Asleep at the Wheel, Alvin Crow and the Pleasant Valley Boys, and other young musicians. The original Playboys had an obvious magnetic appeal. Then came something of a surprise. The band began booking dances at some of the stops on their old circuit and found that the enthusiasm of the older fans matched that of the younger ones. The people who had made up much of their original audience were now responding to the Texas Playboys without Bob's guiding presence. Musically, it made sense. He had trained them so well, they had been schooled so thoroughly in thousands of appearances, and they were, of course, outstanding musicians. But the power of Bob's personal presence was so important that no one knew exactly how people who had seen them under Bob's direction would react to them now that they were playing together without him. The Playboys knew the minute they stepped on a stage after Bob's death that their performances were tributes to Bob. What they hadn't anticipated was how much people who remembered Bob would appreciate getting to celebrate his impact on their lives. In an interview during those years, I asked bass player and vocalist Joe Ferguson what it was like being the Texas Playboys without Bob Wills. He told me, "We're not playing without Bob, not really. I keep looking over my shoulder. It's just like he was on the stand—just the same as if he was there."

One of the most remarkable events occurred in April 1976 at Bob Wills Day, an annual celebration honoring Bob in his hometown of Turkey, Texas. This was the band's first show there since Bob's death the year before. Emotions and expectations were very high. The celebration features a parade and other observances and, of course, lots of music. The Playboys were scheduled to play an afternoon concert at the local football stadium and a dance that night in the high school's gym. The afternoon show was set up on a flatbed trailer and went along well until the last two or three songs. I was there, paying special attention, as always, to the ways Al and drummer Smoky Dacus played together, and I noticed a pained expression on Smoky's face. He would often make funny faces while they played, sometimes to coax Al to "play over his head," but this didn't seem to be that. The look got worse as they neared the end of their last number, the "Texas Playboy Theme." I started to think there was something wrong with Smoky. They hit the last beat on the theme song, and as they all stood to accept the applause, Sleepy Johnson collapsed. He dropped his banjo and lay sprawled near the back of the trailer. Sleepy was the multi-instrumentalist who had started with Bob back in Fort Worth. He played the fiddle in Al and Betty's living room with Bob and Merle Haggard in 1972 and played fiddle and banjo on the *Austin City Limits* recording session in 1975. And, at an earlier Bob Wills Day, he and Bob had performed a heart-breaking number. Bob's right hand had been paralyzed by the strokes, but he wanted to play the fiddle, and so Sleepy pulled the bow while Bob played the notes with his left hand. People who were there that day said it was one of the most extraordinary things they ever saw.

At the 1976 show in Turkey, there was so much hubbub going on at the end of their set that several of the Playboys didn't know Sleepy had collapsed. Fans were coming up for autographs and all the usual greetings and so on. Amid all the confusion, someone called for an ambulance. They took Sleepy to the nearest hospital, but it was too late. There might have been some discussion of whether they should play the dance scheduled for that evening, and someone might have said, "Sleepy would want us to go on." If any of that happened, I wasn't aware of it. The guys just seemed to know they would play the job and make the best of it.

As the time for the dance drew near, the gym filled with people. The acoustics were terrible, and it seemed that no one really understood Leon McAuliffe's announcement before the first number: "We would like to dedicate this dance to our old friend and fellow Texas Playboy Sleepy Johnson, who died here this afternoon at the conclusion of our concert." They started playing, and the music was a little rough at first but quickly evened out. I had managed to get set up on the back corner of the stage so I could watch Smoky and Al, and then I began to feel the stage pulsating. It wasn't the way sound travels when you drop something on a table or the way you can hear music coming from another room. It was as if the stage transmitted the rhythm being played by the band. It had become an instrument itself. Maybe this was common for the Playboys, but I had never experienced it. When the band took a break, Smoky told me what had happened that afternoon. He had gotten concerned during those last songs that Sleepy was losing the beat. For a skilled and experienced rhythm player such as Sleepy to get ahead of or behind the beat was unthinkable, and Smoky knew something was wrong but didn't know what it was. Sleepy was having a heart attack. But he didn't want to stop, call attention to himself, and get some help. He was dying, but the only thing he knew to do was to finish the performance.

Another death that hit hard was the loss of Jesse Ashlock, one of Bob's first fiddlers and the one who was so ornery and full of mischief that Bob kept firing him but who was such a good player that Bob kept hiring him back. He died in August 1976 in Austin, just a few months after Sleepy's death in Turkey. Jesse died on a Monday after playing a job with the Playboys at the Broken Spoke the previous weekend. At that dance, sister Judy took my all-time favorite photograph of Al. He was so happy, with a giant smile on his face and several of the guys in the background of the shot, including Jesse. I couldn't tell that Jesse was even sick that night, let alone a couple of days away from his death. Like Sleepy, he was a total professional who didn't let his problems interfere with the music. The last song of the night was the Glenn Miller megahit "In the Mood," which I don't think I'd ever heard the Playboys perform but which there's every reason to believe they had played many times in the old days. Jesse was one of those fiddlers who often played his instrument like a horn player and gave the band a sound none of the other fiddlers really created. Leon also did that often on his steel guitar. Jesse was crazy about the great jazz violinist Joe Venuti and was a fan of the also-great Stephane Grappelli. Jesse used to talk about listening to Grappelli and Rheinhardt's records in the 1930s and the ways they influenced the Texas Playboys. If you listen to some of the Rheinhardt/Grappelli recordings from those days, you can hear licks that show up in Playboy recordings. I always wished I could have known if the great duo listened to any of Bob's records. If I could have figured out how to get backstage at the one time I saw Grappelli perform, I would have asked him. It was in Austin in the late 1980s. Jim Haber and I went to the show. The first person we saw when we entered the concert hall was Johnny Gimble.

He said, "Every fiddler within five hundred miles of Austin asked for the night off tonight." I'd like to think Grappelli heard Jesse Ashlock play the fiddle. It was fitting that his last song that night at the Broken Spoke, probably the last song he ever played, was "In the Mood," one of the anthems of the Swing Era.

Something else happened that night at the Broken Spoke that seemed a little off. During a break, a guy came up to talk to Al. This was a young fellow, probably about the age I was then. There was a line of folks waiting to talk with Al, and while the guy was waiting, he struck up a conversation with me. I'm sure he didn't have any idea that I was Al's son. He told me he was learning to play the banjo and that he was planning to create a character based on Sleepy Johnson. He knew Sleepy had died some months earlier and said he knew a little about Sleepy's background with Bob, the Light Crust Doughboys, the early days of the Playboys, and that he was planning to call himself "Slappy Johnson." The only thing that kept me from laughing out loud was the fact that I was offended by what seemed like an insult to Sleepy's memory. I managed to get away and find someone else to talk to, and I never knew if he pitched his idea to Al. We never talked about it. Most of the people who really got into the music and the resurgence of interest in the Texas Playboys were respectful of the story and how much it meant to people. Some people, though, were just kind of weird.

•••

When the band got back together in the 1970s, the first few appearances they made featured a couple of bass players with ties to the Playboys but who had not actually worked with Bob, at least not in the '30s. It was great fun to see some of the guys from the 1930s band playing together: "Take It Away" Leon McAuliffe, the famous steel guitarist; Eldon Shamblin, the Playboys' truly legendary rhythm guitarist; Smoky, who had done so much to create the music that came to be called western swing; Sleepy, the multi-instrumentalist who helped create the foundation of this music; Jesse, one of Bob's greatest fiddlers from the early days; and, of course, Brother Al. There was a gap, though, in the reunited band. Everybody knew that Joe Ferguson, one of the Playboys from the 1930s, was still alive, and several of us suggested that Al check to see if he was up to going out with the band. Joe was a remarkable musician. He played bass with the Playboys, giving up his spot from time to time when Bob's cousin Son Lansford, who was also a bass player and a fine musician, needed a job and came onto the band. One of those times, Bob didn't want to ask Joe to leave to make room for Son, and Joe said he had always wanted to play the saxophone, so a couple of guys in the horn section showed him where to put his fingers and how to blow the thing. And off he went. It's almost unimaginable how hard it would be for a novice to pick up a reed instrument and quickly be able to make anything resembling music come out of it, but Joe did it. In fact, he got good enough fast enough to play sax on the most famous western swing recording ever made, the vocal version of "San Antonio Rose." Joe was also a gifted vocalist, what in those days they called a "crooner," and he sang some of the pop hits of the day that Bob liked to include in the band's appearances.

When the guys got back together, they needed a bass player. Joe lived in Fort Worth, and he and Al had kept in touch, so Al knew Joe had had some health problems. But he called Joe to ask if he thought he was up to playing with the reconstituted band. He said he thought he was, and Leon, as leader of the reconstituted band, and the other guys decided to give him a try in Wichita at one of their old regular spots from the circuit they played the first time they were together. The bass player they had been using needed to get back to what he was doing anyway, and Joe was delighted to be asked and did very well. After the show, Smoky got everybody together in the dressing room and made a remarkable speech about what a great job Joe had done that night. It was funny, heartfelt, and convincing, saying in essence that they needed a bass player, that Joe knew all their songs, that he was a great guy, and that they just needed him back in the band. So that's what happened, and that's the way Smoky was. He was one of the only men I ever knew who was completely comfortable expressing his deep love for his friends. Smoky told me in an interview, "Strick and I were always close and knew it, because we played to each other's feelings every night." He once signed a photograph that showed him talking with Al: "To Father—You know I wouldn't listen if I didn't love you." Smoky's affection for Joe and memories of their time together in the old days helped pull Joe back into the band.

Venues along their old dance circuit enjoyed having the Playboys back. The guys in the band enjoyed the reaction they got from young people, but after a lot of these young people moved on to other interests, the folks from the band's first time around were the ones who really meant a lot to the band members. The band and the old fans all got to see each other again and enjoy remembering and re-experiencing how much the music had meant to the people who listened to it and to the ones who created it. Al enjoyed all that a great deal, even when people went overboard with their appreciation. I was with him at a dance in Wichita once when he was desperate to get to the restroom during one of the breaks the band was taking in those days, long removed from the breakless four-hour marathons of Bob's day. People kept stopping Al to greet him and thank him for all the great music and memories. Finally, I realized his "uniform" was giving him away. I said, "Give me your hat." Without his cowboy hat he was able to blend in with the crowd and get to the restroom. He told me when he got out that one of the other men waiting to use the restroom, not recognizing him as one of the Playboys, said, "Those old guys can still play, can't they? Aren't they something!" Al said he responded, "Yes, sir. They certainly are!"

They also played some events that were new to them. The big chili festival in San Marcos, Texas, hosted them ten years, and they appeared several times at the folk festival in Kerrville. One of those appearances was the occasion of a famous episode in our family. I was dating Sally Browder at the time, on the way to becoming engaged. I asked her if she wanted to go to Kerrville and see the festival and the Playboys and meet my dad. Knowing only a little of what might transpire, she bravely said yes. We had arranged to see Al at the band's hotel, and we got there at the appointed time. I saw his car in the parking lot, but he wasn't there. We had been standing outside for a while when suddenly a Volkswagen Beetle came blasting up to the front door of the hotel, being driven by a very young female volunteer from the festival who was shuttling performers to and from the venue and who might have been described as a groupie. There were young people in those days who followed the band around and showed up at various performances, sometimes seeming to have a range of interests, shall we say, in the music and in the musicians. One young fan was a courageous blind woman who hitchhiked, as far as I could tell by herself, to a long string of Playboy appearances. How she managed that baffled me. At this occasion at the hotel in Kerrville, though, Al scrambled out of the VW and the cloud of dust it had created—laughing and waving his arms and thanking his driver for the exciting ride—and met his wide-eyed future daughter-in-law.

•••

When he decided to write his book, *My Years with Bob Wills*, my sister Nancy was a huge help to Al. As she told me in an interview,

> Daddy and I had been talking about writing a book for some time. I wanted the book as much for the future generations of our family as anything. I set up my typewriter on an old library table that [Al's Aunt Cora's husband] Uncle Hub had made and would work at night after the kids went to bed. Daddy would write in notes in long hand, and I would translate and edit it on typewritten sheets. Eventually, he would type his improvisation. Three times I typed various versions of the manuscript with three carbons each time. Merle Haggard wanted a copy as soon as possible. He told Daddy not to worry about form or editing. He wanted to make a movie. Daddy narrated the book on tape and mailed it to Merle. Even with all of our editing and rewriting it was a long way from being polished enough for publication. Daddy was very fond of [*Fort Worth Star-Telegram* writer] Jon McConal and decided to let Jon put the book in final form. The final published book [published by the Naylor Company of San Antonio in 1976] contained a lot of improper grammar and profanity that Daddy didn't normally use.

That the book had some things we didn't care for was a little annoying to the family, but a gigantic disappointment came about eight months after the book came out. Just before Al was to get his first royalty check from the publisher, after having done book-signing events and interviews all over Texas and Oklahoma, Naylor declared bankruptcy. Al didn't comment, as far as I know, on how unfair it was that he had worked so hard to pay off his own business debts back in the '50s and avoid declaring bankruptcy, only to be stiffed by his publisher years later out of what probably would have been the largest check he would have gotten for his book. I went with him to the hearing in the bankruptcy court in San Antonio. He hadn't expected to get rich from sales of the book, but it was a bitter blow. He and the staff of the publisher worked very hard in that first year of the book's life. He did signing events in dozens of places in Texas and Oklahoma, and the book was reviewed in almost a hundred print and broadcast media outlets. One funny thing happened to Betty, after the book came out, when she was filling in as the temporary secretary of the Cleburne Chamber of Commerce and took a call from someone in Abilene who asked, "Can you please give me the address for Mr. Al Stricklin?" Betty said, "You know, I can. You may not believe this, but you're talking to his wife!" Al enjoyed the reactions the book received, such as a letter from a reader and longtime fan in Perryton, Texas, who said, "I can't find the right words to express my feelings. *My Years with Bob Wills* is truly a great book. I shed a lot of tears, page after page. I also laughed so hard, page after page." A fan in Highland, Kansas, wrote to him to say, "I never was so moved by a book in my life. I wiped the tears and read it all at one sitting." He appreciated those messages, but what happened with the book was still a searing disappointment. He got the copyright for his manuscript and re-published it with Eakin Press. Nancy edited the revised version and, as she says, "I corrected the grammar, changed any profanity that I didn't believe was actually part of the story, and corrected a misspelled name."

In 1976, Al accomplished something he'd wanted to do for decades, which was to make a record of his own, playing melody rather than just accompanying other musicians. The result was *Brother Al Stricklin Now*. With Smoky Dacus, of course, providing the beat, and Tommy Alsup on bass and guitar, he recorded Wills/ Texas Playboys songs "San Antonio Rose," "Maiden's Prayer,"

"Faded Love," and "Take Me Back to Tulsa," along with a couple of tunes of his own composition. One of those was a lightning-fast novelty tune he called "Live Bait." He rounded out the album with several pop standards. The Texas Re-cord Company released it. Tommy Alsup was a veteran of the Mark Spitz Water Follies and, more importantly, a noted record producer and the survivor of the luckiest lost coin-toss in American musical history, when, as a member of Buddy Holly's band the Crickets, he gave up his seat on a chartered airplane to Ritchie Valens, who died along with Holly, J. P. Richardson, and the plane's pilot when it crashed in a field in Iowa in 1959. Tommy produced an album of the reunited Texas Playboys that was released by Capitol Records in 1977 and that included a slightly slowed-down version of "Osage Stomp," the frenzied song that was the first thing they ever recorded together, back in 1935. The Playboys also recorded a live album for Capitol, taped at a show at Knott's Berry Farm near Los Angeles before a reported crowd of 16,000. It was released early in 1978 and was the only live album they ever made. They then recorded several albums for Texas-based Delta Records. Because of Delta Records, Al, who made his first money as a musician playing for a silent movie, got to be in a music video. He was probably one of a very small handful of musicians who could say they spanned the time from silent movies to music videos. In 1984, Delta released *75 Years of "Brother" Al Stricklin*, a double album recorded in Fort Worth on his birthday in January 1983 at the Tarrant County Convention Center for Johnnie High's Country Music Revue. The show featured Floyd Domino, Leon McAuliffe, Smoky Dacus, Joe Ferguson, and several other guys Al had played with over the years, including Bobby Boatright, who never played with Bob but who joined the Original Texas Playboys after they went through a bad period of losing fiddlers.

Also in 1984, Al and I and my old historian friend and road buddy Steve Tucker drove to Lubbock to do a program on music for a meeting of the Texas Historical Commission. Al was always trying to lose weight and on this occasion was about a month into one of his regular diets. We stopped at a café somewhere in West Texas and sat down in a booth. A very pleasant waitress approached and told us about the special that day, which was chicken-fried steak with gravy, mashed potatoes, more gravy, some beans, a nice roll, and a piece of pie. Diet-conscious Al said he'd have the special, but no thanks on the pie. The waitress said, "But you might as well get that pie. It comes with the special." Al said, "No. Thank you. I'm trying to lose some weight." Tucker was getting his own pie, so Al asked me if I wanted it, to go along with the hamburger I was planning to have. I said no thanks, that I don't usually have dessert at lunch. I looked up at the waitress and added, "No offense." The waitress said, "That's quite all right, but it's a really good piece of icebox pie. Y'all are paying for it. One of you should get to enjoy it. To tell you the truth, it's really what we're known for." And she pointed over to a cooler where you could behold the pies. Al held fast: "Oh, thank you so much. It looks fine, but I'm not gonna eat it, and I don't want it to go to waste." Then followed an epic struggle. Every time the waitress came by, she'd try to tempt Al with the pie. Every time, he rebuffed her. She came by again, and again. "Don't you want that pie?" "No, thanks all the same." At least a half-dozen times, maybe more. Then we were finished. We sat there a minute longer, talking about this and that and what we were planning to do at the event in Lubbock. Tucker and I would each give a talk, then I'd interview Al for a while, and then he would play the piano and answer questions. It was time to head out for Lubbock. Defeated, the waitress saw that we were ready. She came over with the check, thanked us, and started to turn to walk away, just as Al said, "Ma'am, what's a fella gotta do around here to get a piece of pie."

By the 1980s, the reconstituted band had gotten a lot of attention through several appearances on *Austin City Limits*, a lineup of new albums, and stories in broadcast and print media around the country. They got invitations to play special programs in some interesting venues, including the Smithsonian Institution, and they went to Switzerland in 1983 under the sponsorship of the U.S. State Department. Several of us joked with the guys about the urgent need to establish goodwill with the Swiss and keep us from slipping into conflict with the historically neutral country. The Playboys received a nice welcome and enjoyed the trip, though Al complained that when he asked for a glass of milk at breakfast, it was served warm. He thought that was surprisingly backward, considering how modern the place seemed to be otherwise. The concert at the Smithsonian was a riot, in several ways. While Leon McAuliffe was a very good onstage band leader, he was not a particularly organized person. They would have benefited greatly from having a tour manager. They played all over the place, especially in their old touring radius of Oklahoma, Texas, Kansas, and Arkansas, but also in other places scattered around the country. They never traveled together as a group, just getting themselves to the show however they could. They had three or four uniforms and had to get to the show wearing the right one. They had their instruments to deal with, all except Al, of course. And the way they communicated with each other about how to get all this ready was that Leon would call everybody. On more than one occasion, confusion entered the picture, which is what happened when they played the Smithsonian.

Sally and I were living in Durham, North Carolina, at the time of that show in 1981, and Al called to say we ought to come up to D.C. and see them play and that he would send all the details in a letter. We thought this was all a great idea and invited our friend Brooks

Graebner to go with us. In those pre-internet days, the letter with the details of the show arrived just before we had to leave to drive up to Washington, and we found out when we got there that every detail in the letter was wrong except the day of the show. The letter named the museum where the show would be, but the show wasn't there. It also said the Playboys were staying at the "Lefeant Hotel." We figured that was supposed to be L'Enfant and, because we had gotten there a couple of hours before the (incorrect) time of the show listed in the letter, we had time to find what turned out to be the L'Enfant Plaza Hotel. But the guys had already left to do the sound check at the (still unknown) actual museum. The three of us were standing there wondering what to do when a guy wearing a cowboy hat came walking through the lobby. We figured this had to mean something and stopped the guy and asked if by any chance he was going to see the Texas Playboys. "Well, by golly, I sure am," he said. "I just called a cab. Why don't y'all ride over there with me? The show starts in about twenty minutes!" We got there on time. The show was great. Everybody had a big laugh about the confusion and said, "You know, we really ought to have a tour manager," but they never got one. How they all made it to a show—ever, let alone each time—was always a mystery.

Their appearances became frequent and far flung. Betty's diary for 1983, for instance, has dates for San Antonio; Dallas; Weatherford; Turkey; Fort Smith, Arkansas; Mustang, Oklahoma; Hiawassee, Georgia; Meridian, Mississippi; Wichita, Kansas; three shows in Austin; three in Fort Worth; and, of course, the one in Switzerland.

Judy remembered how chaotic their traveling was, not having a bus and just getting to concerts and dances on their own, especially during one trip to Turkey:

Several members of the family had the experience of driving with Daddy to concerts, chili cook-offs, and Bob Wills Day in Turkey, Texas, each year. Each of us has a story to tell on every trip. My memories of these trips vary from taking him to the airport to catch a plane to driving a carload of the guys back from Turkey to the motel in Childress at 3:30 a.m. The most memorable of those was the trip from Turkey. They had played a dance on Friday night and were to come back the next morning for an all-day celebration capped off by a concert Saturday night. The dance was a great success and shut down at about 1 a.m.

After signing autographs and talking to the last of the crowd about an hour later, Daddy and three of the guys decided to sit down and have a jam session "for a few tunes." They finally quit about three-thirty. Many times, I've wished I'd had a tape recorder for that session. That was some of the best blues/western swing combination I'd ever heard any of them play. By the time I got them in the car, I thought they'd sleep all the way back to the motel. No such luck. They laughed and told jokes and acted like teenagers who were out breaking curfew. Tommy Alsup kept telling me to go faster. [Apparently hoping to recreate the Mark Spitz Water Follies experience, he said,] "I want to take a swim when we get there." Well, those roads are straight as an arrow and very dark and very isolated in the wee hours of the morning, so I stepped on it pretty good. Needless to say, there was one car I passed, a highway patrolman. Of course, I got pulled over. The patrolman didn't buy my story at first, but those four guys kept talking, giggling, and offering him tickets to the concert the next night, and he finally believed I had my hands full just trying to get them all back to the motel alive, so he let me off with a warning. We pulled into the parking lot of the motel around five. No one hit the swimming pool, thank goodness. They all went to their rooms with the agreement of having breakfast together at six-thirty. I thought, "Yeah, right." There was no way these guys in their sixties

> and seventies would be able to bounce back that fast. Surely, they'd sleep until noon. Nope. I was the only one who slept in. They were all through with breakfast and hounding me to get up and take them back to Turkey by eight. Unbelievable.

Turkey provided the setting for one of Al's favorite memories of Johnny Gimble, who had a keen sense of humor. The great fiddler wasn't often able to play with the reconstituted Playboys because of his other commitments, especially the heavy demand for his services as a session player. But on one of the times he was able to join them at Turkey, Johnny was handing out copies of an LP he had recorded, just giving them to anyone who seemed interested in having one. Al saw him and asked, "Johnny, what are you doing?" Without missing a beat, Johnny said, "I'm proving the experts wrong. They told me in Nashville that if I recorded a solo album of fiddle tunes I wouldn't be able to give them away." Johnny once cracked everybody up while they were playing "Bring It On Down to My House, Honey," which had a line in the vocal where one of the guys would say, "Hey, old man, can you play a fiddle?" And the response was supposed to be, "Well, by crackies, I can play a little." But when Johnny was served the line "Can you play a fiddle?" he just said, "I fiddle some."

Nancy's son Robert drove Al to a lot of shows and dances too. All of Al's kids and grandkids are musicians of one sort or another, and Robert's memories of traveling with Al to various jobs often meant something special because of his own musicianship. He recalled another café episode:

> Over a period of several years, in the 1980s, I had the distinct joy of driving my super-cool grandfather to gigs he wasn't necessarily comfortable traveling to alone. As a musician myself, this was beyond awe-

some and allowed me a glimpse into the life of professional musicians far beyond the "garage band" scene I was involved with in the Dallas-Fort Worth area. I absolutely adored my granddaddy, and this was of course time very well spent with him. There was always a healthy dose of serendipity on these trips. One occasion that comes to mind was a return trip back from a Central Texas concert to Cleburne. It was getting a bit late, and the subject of food came up, which was not at all surprising for those who knew AMS. Cruising along I-35, we spotted a roadside truckstop/diner somewhere near Abbott. Granddaddy gave me the nod, and we pulled in. Nice little place, but we were the only people there except for the waitstaff and cook. We were seated and both decided to order a tall stack of pancakes. Why not!

As we waited on our food, one of the waitresses went to a piano against a wall in the dining room and started pecking at the keys. Nothing notable, except for the grin on my grandfather's face. I could tell he was planning some friendly mischief! The other waitress returned with our beverages, and he mentioned the piano playing to her, something like, "She's pretty good." Our waitress replied yes, and Al gently directed the conversation to western swing music and the concert by the Original Texas Playboys earlier that evening down the road. She took the bait and, of all things, mentioned that they loved "that Al Stricklin Piano Pounder"! I thought *Game On. Well Played, AMS!* So he asked the lady if he could have a go at the old piano. They kind of laughed with a little touch of friendly doubtfulness and said sure. He approached the piano and took his seat on the bench. Now we have a little issue. As he sat down, I could plainly see his hand-tooled Piano Pounder belt showing the whole restaurant who had just saddled up to ride! Thankfully, the waitresses hadn't noticed. He plucked and picked around for a moment or two, then cut loose on the keys and really let it rip! The ladies, the cook, and anyone else in the restaurant by then were just blown away.

Sure enough, his belt inscription was spotted, and his identity was blown! There were laughs, tears of joy, and autographs signed. What a sight it was to see this go down! To see the joy in my beloved grandfather's eyes was priceless. He lived for these moments. After traveling with him for several years, I learned never to be surprised by what might happen next, based on his notoriety, his quick wit, and his love for the fans of western swing. This is what it was like to travel with Brother Al Stricklin, my grandfather. And that was probably the best stack of pancakes I ever had.

Nancy often took Al, Joe Ferguson, and Leon Rausch, who all lived in the Fort Worth area, to catch planes at DFW Airport. She recalled picking them up when they came back from the Country Music Association Awards. The band's award was what the CMA calls a "bullet," because of its distinctive shape, but Al called it "the big suppository."

The Playboys had a lot of success and a lot of recognition. They were named Country Music Association Band of the Year and Touring Band of the Year. They were inducted into the Rock & Roll Hall of Fame in the Early Influences category and appeared in the movie *Places in the Heart* in 1984, playing one of two dance bands featured in the story. Al enjoyed visiting with the film's director, Robert Benton, about the fact that Al's mother was a Benton and that he and the famous director and writer, who was born in Ellis County, Texas, were probably kin. Once the band had become so popular, one of my old Cleburne friends, Tom Van Laningham, accosted me for not telling him when we were kids that my dad had played with Bob Wills. By then, the guys from the original band from the '30s had gotten a lot of publicity, with the *Austin City Limits* appearances and the new albums and so on. I just said, "Would it have meant anything to you back then?" Tom said, "I guess not." I said, "Well, there you go." One of my favorite things about the resurgence of Al's career was that he got to play with some younger musicians, including one of my favorite boyhood friends, Michael Jay Dohoney, a fine drummer and vocalist I played with a little in a garage band in junior high. Michael became a professional musician, long removed from our old days playing covers of Monkees and Animals hits. He loved playing with Al, and we all loved the fact that they got to make some music together.

Not many people waste a lot of time feeling sorry for celebrities, but famous people do sometimes have to put up with rude, even threatening behavior. Autograph seekers and others who want a piece of the magic they think fame brings can be bothersome, especially the insistent ones. The members of the Texas Playboys, to a great extent in their time and place, became celebrities because of Bob Wills's persistent practice of calling out their names during performances and on recordings. Because of Bob's insistence that the members of his bands always behave toward fans in patient, generous ways, and because Al happened to be a nice man, Al always seemed glad to see people who wanted to talk with him about the old days, get his autograph or maybe a photo, and spend a few moments with a guy a lot of folks had heard of. Sometimes these moments were kind of funny. A fan came up to him one time and said, "Didn't you used to be Al Stricklin?" He laughed and admitted that he had been. Still was, as it turned out.

Sometimes the moments were more poignant. I was talking with Al during a break at a dance the Playboys were playing at the Longhorn Ballroom in Dallas in the late '70s when a very wobbly, highly inebriated older man came up and engaged him in a long description of another time he'd seen the Texas Playboys and how Al and he had talked about something or other. The train of thought was loose. It mostly involved how Al and several of the other Texas Playboys had hung around talking after a dance in the 1930s. I could tell that Al had no memory of anything the guy was telling about and wanted to get away, probably to go to the bathroom. It went on for so long that I was starting to think the entire break would be taken up in talking with this one guy. Finally, the man with the memories said he had to go and said he'd always appreciate the time they had spent together. Al just said to him, "I'll never forget you, boy." After the man walked off, I asked Al who the man was. He just said, "I have no idea. Just some old guy." But that guy represented the multiple thousands who loved the music Bob and the Playboys played and the connections they felt with the music, what it meant to them. Al's saying he'd never forget him was exactly what the man wanted to hear. And maybe he never did forget him.

Al once got a letter addressed to:

> Al Stricklin
> Any Old Piano in Town
> Cleburne, Texas

What this all meant to people became the greatest message of the reconstituted band. The success and good feelings of the period also did a lot to forge a better relationship between Al and Betty. She was able to go to quite a few of the events, both concerts and dances and celebrity fundraisers and such things. She got a kick out of meeting famous people who came to these events, and she especially enjoyed the trips Betty Wills was able to make with them. The band was included for years in a golf tournament and musical fundraising event put on by Willie Nelson and Darrell Royal, the Texas Longhorn football coach. The same with celebrity golf tournaments put on by the Gatlin Brothers and by western musician and poet Red Steagall. Al achieved something remarkable at one of those events. On one day of one of the tournaments, Al was the celebrity with a foursome of really good golfers, who had the low score for that day. The next day he was with a foursome of not-really good golfers, and they had the high score. During the awards ceremony, Darrell Royal recognized Al for having achieved something, he said, he would have thought was impossible. Al and Betty both got a big laugh out of that. He loved meeting sports figures such as football coach Bum Phillips, who became a good friend. Betty loved meeting actors James Garner and Dennis Weaver and singer Phil Harris and came to feel a lot better about being a "band wife" than she had in the first part of their married life. She started getting notepads and the like with "Mrs. Al Stricklin" on them, which was what a lot of women of her generation did but not something she had done much in earlier years. And, again, she was as crazy about Jim Haber/Floyd Domino as Al was. If only because it brought Jim into our family, Al's experience with the reunited band was a great gift.

Jim told me about how, when he met Al, he realized Al wanted someone in the business to carry on the lessons he had learned. The first time they met, Al asked Jim, "Want me to show you everything I know?"

> That was it. That's how a life-changing moment happened. He had never heard me play a single note, [but] as a piano player, Al treated me as an equal. As a musician, he treated me like a son. When the Texas Playboys recorded *For the Last Time,* Al had me sit next to him on the piano bench as the tape rolled. Al's spirit and guidance were so genuine. He passed the torch to me. He showed me how to play with a rhythm section, how to swing more all the time, how to start a solo with a signa-

> ture trademark, how to enjoy every moment of being a musician, how to treat people, and more.

Jim is too modest in his description of his own talent, but his tribute to Al gives a sense of how the Old Piano Pounder did his work:

> Al and I have different piano styles, and he encouraged me to be myself and play my style. Still, there are times when I can channel Al's spirit in my playing, when people would swear it was Al. After Al passed away, when I played on George Strait's albums, friends would call Betty and tell her they heard Al on the radio with George Strait. She would tell them, "That's Floyd," and they would argue with her and say, "No, I'm sure." It was the ultimate compliment. I did not try to imitate Al. I just thought of that twinkle in his eye, how he bounced on that piano bench. I will never play those octaves as fast and clean as Al or consistently be able to play something exciting and unexpected the way he did or smile that megawatt smile of his or interact with audiences every minute of the show for over fifty years. But I try.

Al and some of the other guys in the band wanted someone to pick up what they had gotten so good at over so many years. Jim said,

> I grew up in California in the 1960s. Growing up in Berkeley I loved the music of my generations and always played the piano, being an avid jazz fan. I attended the Monterey Pop Festival and hitchhiked across the country and made it to Woodstock in 1969. When I joined Asleep at the Wheel in 1972, I had never heard of Bob Wills and had no knowledge of western swing. I loved it immediately, though, and found that Al and the other Texas Playboys welcomed young players. The older players

> were early innovators, and they wanted us to know that it didn't all start and end with them. They let us know that we belonged and that they would always support us and not pass judgment. Today, I try to pass along what I can to young players. Their jaws drop when I tell them Al Stricklin was the one who took me under his wing.

Jim and Al were featured in companion articles in a 1976 issue of *Contemporary Keyboard*: the one on Al by Douglas B. Green—later to become "Ranger Doug" in the famed western group Riders in the Sky—and the one on Jim by Dan Forte. The Doug Green piece gave the most extensive description in print of Al's approach to playing the piano, including his sense of the instrument's role in a rhythm section, and his methods of chord building and the "voicing" of chords. Jim said in the piece about him that "even though Al patterned himself after players such as Earl Hines, he's totally original. He just plays it." Al also paid tribute in the article about him to Fred Calhoun as the first piano player in what became known as a western swing band, Milton Brown's great group, the Musical Brownies.

Jim's importance to our family took a lot of forms. Nancy described one of them, involving the song Al played on the day she was born, when Bob asked him during their daily radio broadcast what he wanted to play for that new baby: "I Can't Give You Anything but Love." Nancy said, "That was the first thing he ever played for me, and it was the last thing he played for me. All the years he had a radio show he would play it for me on my birthday." After Al's death, Jim would call her on her birthday and play it over the phone.

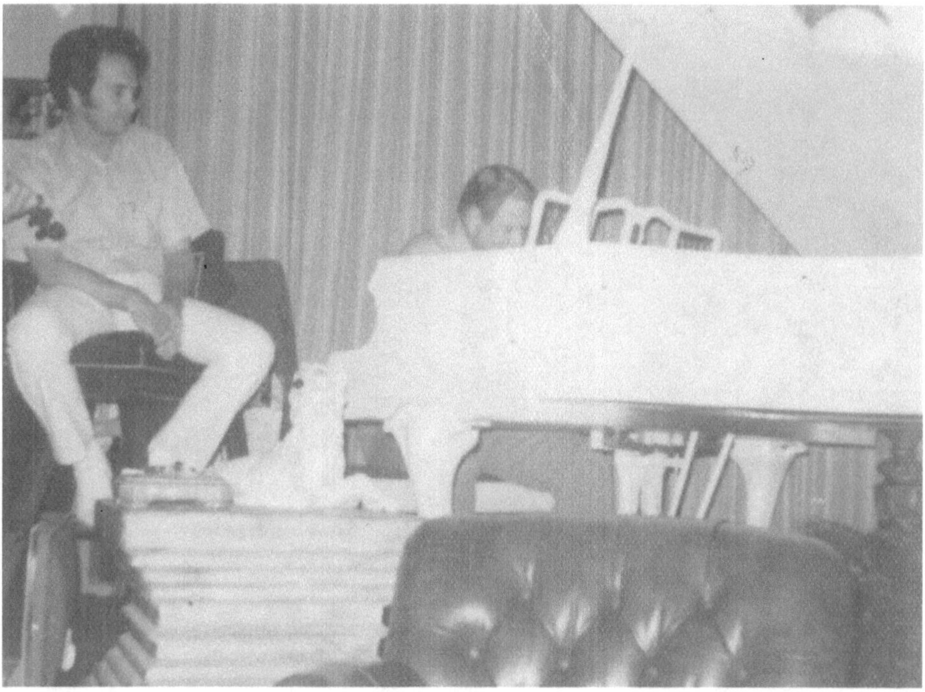

Al playing at Merle Haggard's house in California, 1971.

Bob Wills *(center)* listening to Johnny Gimble and Merle Haggard *(standing, left and right)* and Al (Dick Gimble in the foreground) at Al and Betty's house in Cleburne, 1972.

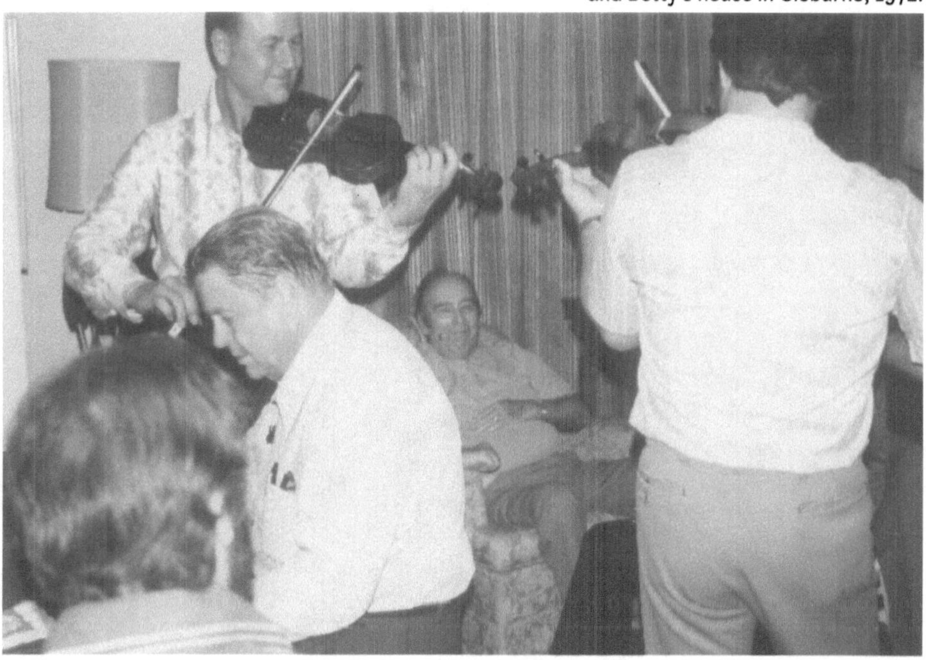

Haggard and Johnny Gimble *(standing, left and right)* with Landa Sloan ("Little Friend Linda"), Betty, and Al and Betty's daughers, Nancy and Judy *(left to right in background)*.

Vernon Solomon, Sleepy Johnson, Betty Wills, Bob Wills, Johnny Gimble *(left to right)*.

Sleepy Johnson, Merle Haggard, Dick Gimble, Johnny Gimble *(left to right)*.

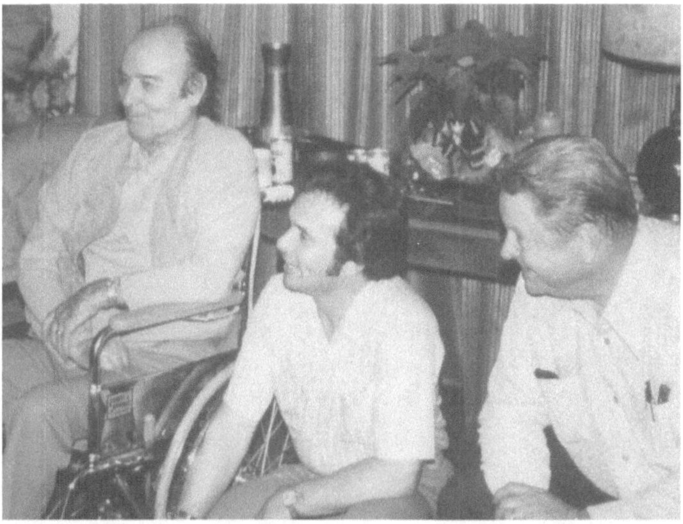

Bob Wills, Merle Haggard, Al *(left to right)*.

Al's sister, Violet, and son, David, playing the piano Violet's parents bought her when she was a child, with one of Al's grandsons, Jerry Carl Willis, looking on.

Al and Smoky Dacus, his dear friend from the original band and the reunited one.

Al at the recording session that produced "Bob Wills and His Texas Playboys: For the Last Time," Dallas, 1973.

Al, Jesse Ashlock, Bobby Boatright, Walter Lyons, Joe Ferguson *(left to right)*, 1976.

Leon McAuliffe, Eldon Shamblin, Joe Ferguson, Al *(left to right)*.

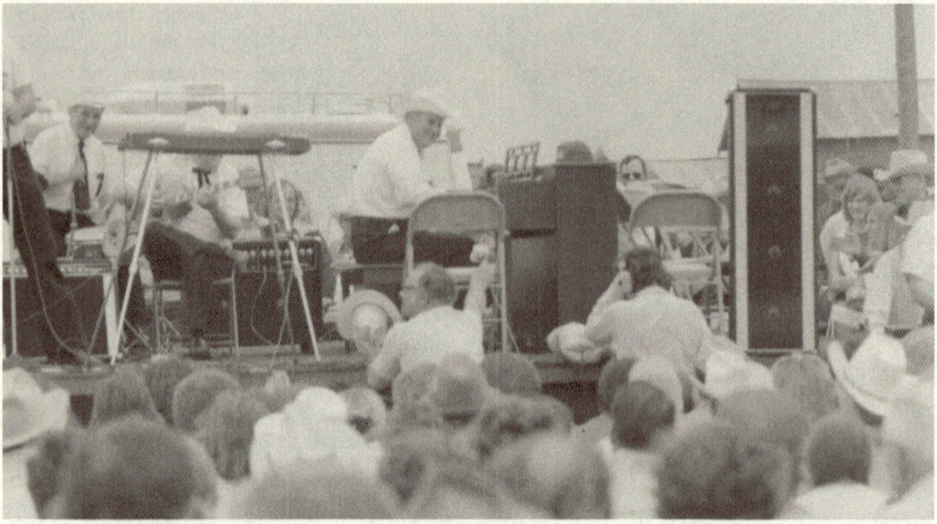

Al and the guys at Bob Wills Day in Turkey, Texas.

Al and Smoky Dacus working on Al's solo album, 1976.

Al greeting fans.

Al and Smoky horsing around.

Al playing with the crowd at the Chilympiad in San Marcos, Texas, 1982.

Al at the Chilympiad.

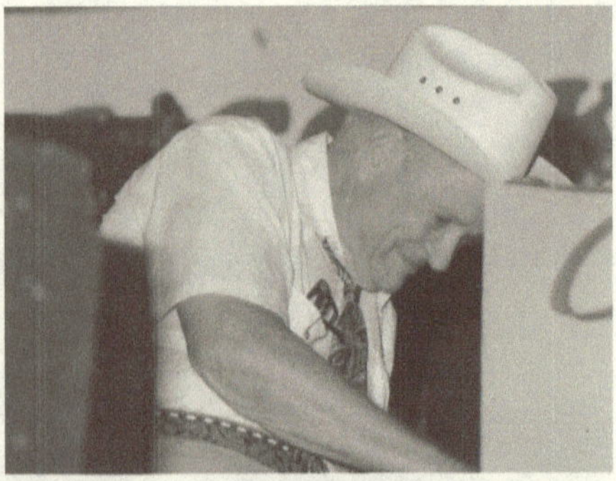

Betty with James Garner and Smoky *(seated)* at the celebrity golf tournament sponsored by Willie Nelson and Darrell Royal, 1983.

Floyd Domino *(at the keyboard)*, Al's great friend and student.

Al and Betty backstage.

Brother Al Stricklin.

CHAPTER 10

Goodbye to a Texas Playboy

Al got sick over the winter of 1985–86. He was never very good about going to the doctor and especially about getting checkups. By early 1986, he started showing signs of prostate cancer, though for several months no one knew that's what it was because he didn't go see anybody about it until it had metastasized. By March, he was feeling pretty awful, dealing especially with severe back pain, and he began talking about missing dates. He went with the band to a show at the San Jacinto Monument for the Texas sesquicentennial of independence observance, but when the time for the show arrived, he was unable to play. He made an appearance at the White Elephant in Fort Worth and suffered badly while sitting on the piano bench. It turned out to be his last public performance. The five remaining guys from the 1930s band—Leon, Eldon, Joe, Smoky, and Al—had made a pact that when any one of them became unable to play they would all hang it up instead of dropping off one by one. The rest of the band played out the remaining dates they had lined up and called it quits. Over the summer, Al got cards and letters from well-wishers, which he appreciated getting, but none more than one he got from an old fan. The man wrote,

> Dear Al: I heard you were sick and just wanted to let you know how much I have loved your music over the years. I was one of those poor people back in Oklahoma during the depression who had so much going against us but Bob Wills and the Texas Playboys would come on the radio and give us a lift. We always felt like Bob and you and the other boys in Bob's band were on our side. And I wanted to say thanks.

Al died on October 15, 1986, and was buried in Cleburne. Smoky, the two Leons, Joe, and several other guys who had played with Al came to the funeral. There was a great assembly of other people from the music business in Texas and other folks from various parts of his life. He would have gotten a kick out of introducing all of them to each other. A few days after the funeral, Betty got a letter from a man who said he

> grew up during the Great Depression in the southern part of Limestone County, Texas (the birthplace of Bob Wills), and the two persons admired most in our area were Franklin D. Roosevelt and Bob Wills. I never knew there was any other kind of music except "Bob Wills Music"; in fact, "Faded Love" will be played at my services.

The City of Cleburne put up a historical marker about Al in Hulen Park next to a gazebo. People still talk about him, about the band, about Bob. The joy they gave people, the release, if only for a few hours, from the sense of troubles people felt, the inspiration to get out in public and do your best to entertain folks, to be willing to risk failure in trying to do something truly remarkable on stage—these were gifts that won't soon be forgotten. A Texas State Senate Resolution adopted in Al's memory in February 1987 reads, "[His] music brought joy and happiness to so many people." The guys had one more job scheduled after Al's death that they felt they needed to honor, in Fort Worth, appropriately enough, where so much of this story had begun. They did the show at the Will Rogers Auditorium on November 15, one month to the day after Al's death, with a substitute piano player. I couldn't bring myself to go.

•••

Al had seven great years with Bob Wills when he was in his twenties and thirties, helping create some legendary music and being part of countless stories—playing dances and being on the radio and making records and visiting in people's homes and playing for the funerals of their loved ones and bumping along those wretched roads and having to get back to Tulsa to start the process over every day. He had a long time away from the Texas Playboys, from the early 1940s when the original band broke up because of the war until the middle of the 1970s when the guys from Bob's first band got back together. During that middle period, his life went from okay to not so great to okay again and then to pretty great from 1975 to 1986, when he got to relive the magic Bob had created for them all. He made a lot of new friends, reconnected with some old ones, and got to be part of some fun events such as the celebrity golf tournaments and trips all over the place. That was all great. And even if he hadn't gotten the second experience with the band, he would have survived, though I doubt for as long as he did. But the second time around gave him a chance to be part of something maybe equally important, what amounted to a Bob Wills Appreciation Tour. It's unlikely that any of the guys ever walked up to Bob when they were in the band the first time and said, "I just want to tell you how much I appreciate what you have done, creating this band, making this great music, and letting me be a part of it." But they did that every time they played during that second go-around. I know they felt his presence. And when someone would say, "Brother Al Stricklin now," as Bob had said so often when he wanted Al to play a solo, I suspect Al heard those words as though they were being spoken by Bob himself. It was a great gift to be part of Bob Wills and His Texas Playboys the first time. He knew that as well as anyone and talked and wrote about it, but he thought it really was something on the order of miraculous to be able to do it again.

A lot of people in a lot of places had a lot to do, both the first time and the second time, with the ways the Texas Playboys got to play the music and tell the story of Bob Wills. Bob and the guys in the band touched the lives of many people, both those they met and knew and those they never could have known around the country and to some extent around the world. That all happened largely because this music helped people feel a sense of belonging to a community larger than the little patches of land in which most of them lived out their lives. I said in a piece I wrote in 1993, "It made poets out of plowboys." During the band's first go-round, the music gave people whose lives were dreadfully hard the grace to glide across dance hall floors, borne along by the melodies and rhythms of Bob Wills and the Texas Playboys.

The joy they created both the first time and the second time and the inspiration they gave younger musicians who are still keeping their musical legacy alive extended from people long dead to people not yet born. Young people who will discover this music someday will know that the times, places, and events that gave rise to it and the people who played it must have been truly remarkable. The man at the dance in Wichita said of the Texas Playboys, "Aren't they something!" They were indeed. Brother Al Stricklin certainly was.

ABOUT THE AUTHOR

David Stricklin is a writer and historian, concentrating on southern music and religion. He grew up in a musical family in Cleburne, Texas, and attended Baylor University, where he was trained in oral history and public history. He received a Ph.D. in U.S. history at Tulane University under Bill C. Malone and taught history at Lyon College in Batesville, Arkansas, before becoming director of the Butler Center for Arkansas Studies in Little Rock.

www.ingramcontent.com/pod-product-compliance
Lightning Source LLC
LaVergne TN
LVHW091305250826
846436LV00026B/259